UNDERSTANDING THE EUROPEAN CONTENT INDUSTRIES

Understanding the European Content Industries

A Reader on the Economic and Cultural Contexts of Multimedia

Edited by

Peter A. Bruck

Proceedings of the EUROPRIX Scholars Conference 1999, Tampere, Finland

IOS
Press

Ohmsha

Amsterdam • Berlin • Oxford • Tokyo • Washington, DC

ISBN 1 58603 290 9 (IOS Press)
ISBN 4 274 90548 9 C3055 (Ohmsha)
Library of Congress Control Number: 2002112877

Publisher
IOS Press
Nieuwe Hemweg 6B
1013 BG Amsterdam
The Netherlands
fax: +31 20 620 3419
e-mail: order@iospress.nl

Distributor in the UK and Ireland
IOS Press/Lavis Marketing
73 Lime Walk
Headington
Oxford OX3 7AD
England
fax: +44 1865 75 0079

Distributor in the USA and Canada
IOS Press, Inc.
5795-G Burke Centre Parkway
Burke, VA 22015
USA
fax: +1 703 323 3668
e-mail: iosbooks@iospress.com

Distributor in Germany, Austria and Switzerland
IOS Press/LSL.de
Gerichtsweg 28
D-04103 Leipzig
Germany
fax: +49 341 995 4255

Distributor in Japan
Ohmsha, Ltd.
3-1 Kanda Nishiki-cho
Chiyoda-ku, Tokyo 101-8460
Japan
fax: +81 3 3233 2426

Dedicated to

Peter Kowalski

Contents

Preface of the Editor

"Understanding the European Content Industries" is an international and multidisciplinary reader with a clear focus on multimedia economics and content creativity. The reader covers two main fields of analysis: (a) the economic perspectives of the European content industry and of market developments; and (b) the cultural and educational contexts of multimedia.

The articles are based on academic papers from researchers and scholars with various backgrounds in media and communication research, journalism, sociology, computer sciences and education. Other contributions are from industry advisers, policy analysts and experts working for key European institutions.

Within the last years the content industry has become a major economic growth sector that is fundamentally shaping modern economy, society and culture. Clearly, this development will continue and the new media and emerging content industries will become even more important in the new millennium.

The reader provides analyses of key issues in this development through the high academic quality of the contributions, its international and multidisciplinary approach as well as the topicality of the findings. The book can be used as reference book on the issues surrounding new media and as textbook in multimedia classes at universities and other institutions of higher learning. However, it mainly addresses the advanced reader who has professional ambitions and personal interests in the multimedia business (either as an academic or as a practitioner).

The book provides readers with both an analytical, academic and a practical business view on various economic, cultural and societal issues of the European multimedia content industries. The articles review and re-evaluate existing research and demonstrate new insights into economic and analytical problems of new media. The book assists the readers in gaining a more circumspect view of the possibilities and challenges in multimedia and introduces them to the main issues of these new markets.

The book originates from the EUROPRIX Scholars Conference, which was held for the first time in November 1999 in Tampere in Finland. The event is developing into a regular scholarly conference concerned with the development of the multimedia and content industries in Europe. This conference will be organised annually in the context of the EUROPRIX contest and its related activities. Scholars, researchers, multimedia producers and industry people are invited to present papers for discussion and debate.

Research presented is chosen for its contribution to the economic analysis of current multimedia development and new business strategies in the content industries, to the cultural analysis of trends in information society contents and applications, and to the legal, regulatory and political aspects of well-functioning information markets, content production and trading. Papers on technological developments are welcome in as much as they contribute to the understanding and debate of the economic, cultural, legal and political issues.

The conference is the outcome of the discussion of the expert jury of the EUROPRIX Contest in the last years. The basic idea is simple: in 1999, for instance, 44 multimedia experts spent up to 7 days looking at 442 products from 28 countries in order to evaluate them and judge the best. The intellectual effort going into this evaluation should not be lost, but – to use a multimedia term in a different context – re-purposed for further reflection and systematic analysis of the development of the European information markets. Therefore, jurors have established a framework for collaboration in form of the EUROPRIX Scholars Network. This is fitting because the EUROPRIX initiative itself is the outcome of a study undertaken to analyse the development of electronic publishing.

I want to thank the local organisers of the EUROPRIX Scholars Conference for their work. Specifically, I am indebted to Prof. Jarmo Viteli from the Hypermedia Lab at the University of Tampere and his staff. They were inspiring hosts and made everyone want to return.

Selecting contributions for the conference and soliciting articles was done by Hannes Selhofer, who has honed his skills in various content industry-related studies and publications. The collaboration with him has been a source of great professional joy over the years and much of my writing output is based on his excellent research.

The manuscript in its final form was edited by Tanja Greil. I thank her for her diligence and patience with the texts and with me as the editor.

Salzburg/Ottawa   Peter A. Bruck

Understanding the European Content Industries
P.A. Bruck (Ed.)
IOS Press, 2002

Understanding the European Content Industry. Closing the Value Gap in e-Content
Peter A. Bruck, Austria

A decade ago, the collision between publishing and computing took mainly place on the desks of people. PCs and workstations became powerful and inexpensive enough for all users to start using their desktop for publishing in one or the other way. At the same time, the transformation and broadening of the publishing and computing industries started to take hold. People working in both industries knew that considerable changes would take place, new markets would be developing and old ones not be left unchanged. Today, we speak of content industries combining publishing, but also integrating broadcasting, video, educational institutions or cultural agencies.

The changes effecting the industry happened more quickly than many industry experts forecasted and more slowly than many feared. While the structure and nature of publishing has changed profoundly, making money in these markets remains underdeveloped. Those companies that were the important proprietary suppliers of equipment and systems of the industry a decade ago are mostly gone now. Their place has been taken by a new generation of software and hardware companies and of publishers is claiming their territory. The publishing and broadcasting industries shifted from a situation where proprietary supplier industries served them to a world where the publishing industry depends on what is going on in computing.

The revolution is closely connected to the permeation of desktop computing and the Internet. And the revolution has not stopped since it started. It is an ongoing revolution. The information side is accelerating and the communication side is developing. We have only accustomed ourselves to the cycles of ever increasing computing power at ever reduced costs, but we are not yet able to clearly see what this means to network power. We find ourselves only at the beginning of the online age.

This book addresses the changes in the economic and cultural contexts for the emerging European content industry. This industry emerges out of the increasing convergence of technological platforms (the success of the Internet Protocol), appliances (the PC as a near universal access tool) , of companies and industries (publishers also becoming broadcasters, telecom operators also starting publishing businesses), and of users (interested in using the few brands they have grown to trust). The content industry is booming. But many forget that it took long to get it started, even technologically. And that there is still a long way to go, especially economically, since it remains unclear what constitutes value in the digital content markets. The multimedia and, particularly, the internet economy is struck by an economic paradox: The market values of companies continue to rise while consumers grow increasingly used to not paying for new products and applications provided by these companies. In the area of content, one can find what I call the "value gap": Users demand continuously improved services and new technological functionalities but few to none can say what value they would give to it in monetary terms.

The market will continue to be revolutionised by three technological drives. Yet, the value question will stay the same.

Three driving forces influencing the dynamics of the industry[1]

- **Information revolution**

We know since having read or listened to Gordon Moore, the prescient former chairman of *Intel Corp.*, that computing power doubles every 18 months for half the price: the increase of computing power is not a linear function, it is an exponential function.

What made Gordon Moore's statements from about 35 years ago so dazzling was his prediction of how the marvels of integrated electronics would be engineered over time. He included a graph into his by now famous journal article. With the year on the horizontal axis and the log of the number of components in an integrated circuit on the vertical axis, the graph mapped just four data points: the number of transistors on integrated circuits in 1962, 1963, 1964, and 1965. These points produced an almost straight diagonal line at 45 degrees across the graph, indicating that the number of components had doubled every year, beginning with 2^3 or 8 transistors, continuing with 2^4, and up to 2^6 or 64 transistors. Moore boldly extended the line through to 1975 when 2^{16} or 65,000 transistors would be inscribed on a single chip. This feat was achieved in the designated year in a lab at IBM and got into the consumer market shortly after.

If Moore's law were a mere oddity in the ongoing advance of technology, it would be an extraordinary one, but it is more: What has come to pass is a dynamic where the unprecedented changes in computational power are not a blip in tech development but a broadly sweeping beginning. From processors to storage capacity, from memory to screen displays, every technology touched by integrated electronics has advanced at a radically new speed. Today, the 18-month-pace of Moore's law appears almost slow compared to the three times faster rate of the advance in optics. This takes us to the second driver of the development: Communications.

---

[1] For some of the thoughts in this section I am indebted to George Gilder and Jonathan Seybold.

- **Communications revolution**

As with information processing power we are experiencing a similar development with network power. New transmission technologies and new protocols combine in a dynamic which equals the 18-month-law and its economic impact in halving costs.

Fibre-optic technology and wavelength division multiplexing are emerging as the spearhead of global industrial progress and are fundamentally changing the economics of network connectivity. The new technologies use the different "colours" of light as transmission channels, each bearing billions of bits per second on a single fibre thread of the width of a human hair. A measure of the technology's advance is lambda-bit kilometres, multiplying the number of wavelengths (lambdas) by the data capacity of each and the distance each can travel without slow and costly electronic regeneration of the signal. In 1995, the state of the art was a system with 4 lambdas, each carrying 622 MB per second some 300 kilometres. Three years later, a company announced that it will introduce a 280-lambda system in short order, with each lambda bearing 10 GB per second over a distance of 3,000 kilometres. This will be an 11,000-fold advance in five to six years. With several hundred fibres now sheathed in a single cable, a fibre installation in the next three years or so might be able to carry more than a month's worth of Internet traffic in a single second.

These processes move forward from the seminal effects of Moore's law and the collapse of the price of computation.

There are two results to be considered: an economic and a technical one. In economic terms, the deployment of information processing power is lifted out of the paradigm of scarcity. That is, it is more economical (i.e. rational in economic terms) to waste computational capacity than to spare and save it. This means that the use of IP power will spread into all areas of human life and economic activity. In terms of publishing it means that all will be "multimediarised" in one way or the other.

Technically, the power of microelectronics spreads intelligence through machines, sector by sector, and the power of communications diffuses intelligence through networks – not just computer networks but through companies, societies, and the global economy. A broad dematerialisation will transform all processes and complete the way which was started with the introduction of semiconductors. Photonic carriers can multiply without weight in the same physical space. Virtually any number of colours can occupy the same fibre core. The new optics feed on the ultimate low-entropy carrier – the perfect sine waves of electromagnetism – and can plunge down curves of experience without mass or resistance through worldwide webs of glass and light. We will experience the *grid* still in our lifetime and much sooner than most think or expect.

On a more mundane level: The introduction of broadband networking services to all offices and homes will take place in the next five to seven years and telcos, cable-TV companies, and PCS will compete for the markets.

The Internet architecture has made its way into every household and every office and has changed personal lives and corporate businesses. Today the telecommunications, broadcasting, publishing and entertainment industries are only facing the beginnings of this change, with other social sectors such as educational institutions and government not being far behind. Computers around the world for all kind of purposes are now being knitted into an almost homogenous, interconnected system. This connectability has never been contemplated before and will drive all content provision in the future.

- **Link and interactivity revolution: From product to service**

For ages, publishers worked with pages and books, paragraphs and titles. Through all the changes of technologies and genres, one thing remained the same: There was always a definite beginning and end to the text and, thus, a clear circumscription of the size and volume of what was to be published. Authors delivered their editable and then printable material in a linear structure. Linearity is deeply structural for publishing in the material age. Additionally, publishers and authors knew one other thing: readers had to follow the paths they described or set out. The coming of the electronic age in publishing changed this deep structure and opened up the texts to two revolutionizing forces: the link and the click.

The link stands for the new type of publishing material: the hypertext. Conceived in the 1960s, it was worked on at Brown University in the 1970s, but basically laid dormant for a long period of time. The computer company *Apple* brought hypertext to public awareness in the early eighties when they introduced hypercards which linked functions within a single desktop computer.

Hypertext carries this function of links much further and allows to open up all texts by referencing a potentially unlimited number of other text units with it. In the end webs of information that extend beyond one computer and include large computer networks and a potentially infinite number of libraries can be created.

The invention of the World Wide Web brought the hypertext concept to the world at large and the invention of the Web browser "Mosaic" made hypertexts usable by general users who were no computer freaks. It is fair to say that the Internet could only develop in its deep structure as a truly open information network through the invention of the hypertext.

Hypertext is a completely different way of looking and using texts and information; it makes electronic documents entirely different from print documents. With hypertext electronic documents do neither have a beginning nor an end and texts are not restricted to linearity, but can be skipped, re-visited etc. Users don't have to follow a pre-determined path, but they have the option to switch paths and create their own ways through the world of information. It will still take some time until we will be able to have the help of intelligent agents which track our hypertext paths and interpret the links we choose and recommend to us tracks which we might not have seen or taken or which even authors might not have envisioned.

Publishers and authors, journalists and publicists have, for the first time, to consider the reader beyond the descriptive characteristics which they hold from them. Readers can become partners and clients of more than just one text. And the product of publishing can be transformed into an ongoing, intelligent service which can be personalised and adjusted to readers and their interests.

Electronic documents do not do everything better than what print documents can do. There *is* future in print publishing, but electronic publishing can do well in areas where print documents run up against the limitations of the material product world. Electronic documents do not just transport and present information, they link it and are, thus, the key to what is happening now on the Internet and the WWW.

The outcome of this revolution is not clear. Many things are happening at the same time and the industry landscapes are changed by convergence of technologies and applications. They bring new publishing forms, new businesses, new ways of dealing with information, new commerce and new models to the fore. Right now, the industry is searching models which make the use of hypertext also economically viable. The openness of the electronic product/document might excite the user, for the publisher it opens a Pandora's box of economic questions and threats.

Today, the world of electronic publishing is still built on the models of material publishing: CD-ROMs and other shrink-wrapable products can be economically handled and produce clearly manageable revenue streams; customers pay for the item, be it between covers or in a box; they take delivery in a clear way; they walk out of a store with the product or arrange shipment; and they can return the product if it turns out to be faulty or disappointing. The world of material publishing goods has many givens which need yet to be transposed into the electronic online world. The hypertext revolution will have gained a phase of normality only when customers know exactly what they pay for and agree to the how.

The people who work in electronic publishing right now are still inventing the future. There is no doubt that the Internet is transforming publishing: no matter what publishing companies do in the future, the landscape in which they operate will be changed irrevocably by the Net, and publishing on paper is going to exist in an environment where print publishing will only be one mode of selling, delivering and distributing information.

At the same time, publishing is transforming the Net. The World Wide Web is making information public on a global scale. With WWW the Internet has found its killer application, and hypertext publishing and e-mail are the key drivers of the Net's growth.

But there is still a lot of fear and a lot of anguish among publishers in Europe, among the old and traditional ones as well as among the new and technologically progressive ones. Things change so rapidly.

The old and traditional publishers see themselves surrounded by a lot of hype and insist that they need to know what the return on an investment is in real terms, i.e., sales, revenues and profits. The new and technologically progressive see themselves surrounded by a lot of scepticism and insist that they need to have the chance to develop the new markets and position their companies strategically in future terms, i.e., innovation, new products and new business. In the end, it comes down to two camps: Pro-Net publishing experts and Anti-Net publishing experts.

The Anti-Net people feel mostly threatened by what is happening: Paper is not going to go away, but the Net is transforming the very nature of publishing. They see it all around themselves. There are new players on the markets, fortunes are made by newcomers, there are new rules and the stock markets become an important reference point. They sense that the new people might also determine who the successful new players are and what the fortunes and rules will be.

The Net-partisans see the tide going their way – for the moment: They are convinced that the Net has been the most important invention in publishing and information distribution since the invention of the printing press, and they see a period full of opportunities ahead. For them, the Net is virtually everything: Homestead and market, meeting place and innovation horizon. Other problems of society and economy have receded for them: The Net is close to a panacea. It will transform all distribution of information, business and commerce and, thus, all society. But many of the pro-Net people also know that important questions have still not been answered, the most important of which being: What is value? And how can real income be generated from users willing to pay for advantages of these new forms of publishing?

The value question: What is quality and what is the users' advantage?

Today, the notion of "content" is moving centre stage. Electronic documents are enriched by graphics and images and video can be linked like any other electronic text or document. The term "content" is used to give name to the information units which receive certain media shapes and forms in production and distribution. Content is commercialised in assets which can be traded on the digital marketplaces. Small and big companies from old and new industries are interested in content. They cross-market it, merchandise it, cross-publish and use the convergence of technologies to increase their business opportunities. Contents give usefulness to the Net and the new media, and sustainability to the industries, be they from the entertainment or telecom business.

Multimedia technology is booming and its applications are available in almost all fields of science, commerce, education and leisure time. Yet, ever improving technical features and ever increasing performance sell only the hard- and software of electronic publishing, not the content. In fact, for the publishing business they are insufficient for market success. Consumers need to know what they can do with those gadgets after the first phase of novelty and excitement. What is in demand are quality applications and products. While with print some books might fascinate through their smell or the texture of their pages, it is finally the content which sells. Content in the form of texts and picture fulfil the demand.

Excellence in added value for users

There are a number of ways to establish what constitutes success in the use of the new electronic publishing technologies. One would be to use the mere sales statistics as a guide. However, purchases are often not the results of the excellence of a product but of the amount of marketing Euros spent.

Another is the use of expert judgments and evaluations. In 1998, the biggest such effort was started in Europe with the EUROPRIX Contest[2]. The underlying idea was simple: The developments in publishing have gained such speed and the economic context and business models are so much in flux that only the identification of the best examples of the use of new technologies can be a reliable guide to future developments and the true potential of the new publishing media.

The EUROPRIX Contest built on the practical experience gained by the organisation of a national contest in Austria in the years before. But more importantly it used the insights from the study on the "Future Developments of the Electronic Publishing Industry in Europe", which I had undertaken together with Thomas Baubin for the European Commission two years earlier. In that study we identified the need not just for new business models but for demonstrating the added value of multimedia to readers/users in Europe. We suggested that in online publishing only those publishers would have a chance to succeed in the long run who were able to integrate content with community and commerce, transpose the offline brand into the online market and deliver a premium service in contrast to all the other information so readily available on the Net.

EUROPRIX condensed this analysis and addresses the development of the new publishing with its focus on the value added for users through multimedia. In the EUROPRIX Contest, products are evaluated in terms of their excellence in serving the specific user needs of learning or empowering citizens. EUROPRIX evaluates the best multimedia products and applications on all platforms, whether

---

[2] Cf. http://www.europrix.org

online or offline.

- **Selecting quality: Independent expert judgement**

For users, the selection of high-quality products is a hard job, which is getting harder with the overflowing mass of e-content products and websites. With the growing content output, the transparency of the market for the individual consumer decreases.

Therefore, every year EUROPRIX invites international multimedia experts as jurors for the contest to select Europe's best multimedia products from a pool of 400 to 500 online and offline products which entered the contest. Jurors provide their expertise as producers, marketing experts, journalists, academics, and consultants in all kinds of e-content fields and provide a state-of-the-art assessment of e-content products.

EUROPRIX has developed relevant strategic methods to evaluate the entries professionally and independently. Much time during the usually five days of the jury process are spent in discussions: "What makes the jury unique is definitely the seriousness with which the contest is taken by the jury, the way we work, watch and discuss everybody's ideas and opinions. And finally, I'm convinced that's the best award in that sense that jurors act fully independently and everybody takes an agreement to deeply discuss their evaluation in order to select the best product", says Xavier Berenguer, Director of the Audiovisual Institute at the Pompeu Fabra University of Barcelona, Spain, and member of the EUROPRIX 2001 Jury.

Media theorist Giaco Schiesser, also being a EUROPRIX Jury member, adds that "for the jury, innovation is the main thing to consider – innovation in technical ways, content-wise and under design aspects. The primary criterion is content – Is there new content provided?; then the attractiveness of the product; thirdly, its usability; and finally the overall criterion, how the product is made to be handled by the users."

- **Meeting users' demands**

The EUROPRIX categories address the use of new media in different contexts and for different purposes. They reflect different interest foci as well as lifestyles:

(1) **Knowledge, Discovery and Culture**
    addressing the interests and needs of people willing to learn in all fields of exploration and learning, including science.

(2) **Learning and e-Education**
    looking for products and applications supporting learning and serving the needs of schools, continuing education and the e-learning communities.

(3) **Interactive Fiction and Storytelling**
    entertaining users with captivating digital stories, including games.

(4) **E-Business and Supporting SMEs in e-Business and the Marketplace**
using multimedia for companies and commerce with special attention to multimedia for those 99% of all European companies which give work to 500 Europeans or less.

(5) **Mobile Multimedia**
providing new contents for people on the move and supporting mobility in cars, public transport and via mobile devices including phones.

(6) **Citizens, Democracy and e-Government: Empowerment and Improvement**
using new media for the interests of citizens in all relations with government and public administrations.

(7) **First Steps and Bridging Society with Multimedia**
opening new media to new user groups and serving social cohesion and community building.

- **Creating visibility for quality contents**

EUROPRIX addresses the marketing grid-lock which many producers face in Europe. Offline products face the challenge of distribution, online applications of making themselves known in the information ocean of the Internet. EUROPRIX creates market visibility for high quality content and the possibility to step into the market and gain Europe-wide recognition for the best products.

EUROPRIX has developed an elaborate marketing plan for "Europe's Best in Multimedia" as the award for nomination and winning. Beginning with the official announcement at the Frankfurt Book Fair, the nominees have the opportunity to present their products at the world's largest content fair. They can meet potential sales partners, customers or publishing houses. As the Frankfurt Book Fair continues to be the biggest marketplace for licence trading for books and digital media, producers can make new publishing contacts. For many of the smaller companies it would not be possible to afford this without being a EUROPRIX nominee.

Producers not belonging to the nominees in all categories also gain advantage from the EUROPRIX marketing activities at the Frankfurt Book Fair. They are included in the licence database of the fair showing all the information provided as if they would be an exhibitor. All EUROPRIX participants have the opportunity to be in this database. Additionally, the EUROPRIX publishes the EUROPRIX Licence Rights Catalogue, which is the lexicon of licence rights trading. Since 2000 the catalogue includes a CD-ROM for quick search and added information.

The nominees are presented in a broad media mix (digital, analogue, audio-visual, and print) which is distributed Europe-wide. Additionally, there are a number of presentation events throughout Europe in co-operation with EUROPRIX's Associated Partners, an extensive and growing network of national contact points supporting the promotion of EUROPRIX.

These unique efforts are of greater value to the nominees than a cash award as they get the chance to establish themselves in European markets and start a top career. This is also true for the nominees and winner of the Students Award showcased as Europe's TopTalent during the TopTalent Festival in Vienna.

- **Addressing the whole of Europe**

The EUROPRIX idea, however, covers much more than the selection and promotion of Europe's best multimedia products. EUROPRIX provides a meeting point for co-operation and partnership for multimedia industries all over Europe. To serve this goal EUROPRIX is developing its network year by year. Participants from, e.g., Cyprus, Bulgaria or Ireland gain partners and options for distribution in multimedia markets such as France, Germany or the UK.

Since 1989, Europe is no longer split in East and West along the lines of opposing political systems, but Europe is far from an integrated cultural space or open market for the access to and exchange of cultural products. With the EU currently being comprised of 15 countries in the South, North and West, people and cultural producers including digital publishers in Central and Eastern Europe face enormous barriers. And even within the EU, it is still a long way for an open exchange of cultural "goods". The barriers of language remain high and cultural inflections require considerable efforts in the localisation of multimedia products and applications. In economic terms, this constitutes a market failure.

EUROPRIX has addressed this from the start and invites producers and designers from 33 countries, as well as more than 1,400 schools and institutions offering multimedia training and education to participate. Entries to the contest come from Lithuania and Poland as well as from Turkey and Israel or Portugal and Norway.

- **Establishing a Europe-wide e-content platform and strengthening national multimedia markets**

The central intention of the Austrian EU presidency in 1998, during which EUROPRIX was initiated with the support of the European Commission DG (XIII) Information Society, was to establish a platform bridging East and West, North and South in Europe. Over the years, this has been realised in multiple ways as EUROPRIX has developed into a well-established platform for the exchange of experience between multimedia producers and users. It addresses both the economic and the cultural contexts of new media contents, as is also reflected by this reader. It is conducive to a Europe-wide economic network:

- by supporting small and medium-sized multimedia companies to develop their activities, providing Europe-wide promotion and a marketing push through being selected as nominees and winners;

- by its focus on added value of multimedia products and applications for users;

- by providing an overview of high quality multimedia products across Europe and its richness of choice;

- by making clear what quality is in multimedia;

- by overcoming the boundaries of national markets and language barriers;

- by developing co-operations of over 180 organisations in 33 countries.

Strengthening multimedia markets assures a new cultural industry which supports the ethic, social, integrative or political objectives of the European community. Producers in smaller countries have a considerable creative potential, their products carry the originality of rich cultural heritage and, thus, provide potentially interesting content for users in other parts of Europe as well. In the context of world-wide competition many European multimedia markets, however, are too small for market success on an international level. EUROPRIX supports the integration of smaller multimedia markets and gives producers additional access to a broad European stage. EUROPRIX facilitates a diversity of market structures in Europe, markets that co-operate and, therefore, strengthen themselves making European multimedia industries more competitive in overseas markets.

Connecting with the future: Closing the value gap

Technologies and industries go through rapid and profound changes. This book addresses them. At the same time, contents change to a much slower extent and stories remain structurally unchanged over long periods of human history. Only in a rear view mirror will we be able to say how the economic and cultural contexts of multimedia with their different pace have changed. In the following articles you will find some rich thoughts and well-grounded arguments to guide you when trying to understand the European Content Industry.

The key challenge will be how to close the value gap. The authors of this book contribute from the vastly different perspectives to this question while EUROPRIX tries to provide very pragmatically a mechanism to do so.

Section A

Producing Multimedia. Multimedia Economics and New Business Models

A. Producing Multimedia. Multimedia Economics and New Business Models

1 Overcoming Traditional Media Economics in the Era of Multimedia. A Prospective Methodological Case Study
Gerd G. Kopper, Germany

1.1 Goals and Methods of this Study

This paper starts off with a summary of ongoing analyses of the implication of traditional media economics on strategic thinking within the newspaper industry. A traditional type of economic thinking centred on media and media markets, specifically in terms of daily products is still governing the local and regional newspaper industry. This type of thinking is in stark contrast to a newly evolving type of information economics adequate for an era of multimedia communication industry (cf. Carveth/Owers/Alexander 1998). The contrast and differences between these two types of thinking can be brought into clearest expression in a regional and/or local context.[1]

Basic insights of analyses used for this overview are derived from economic studies of standard product lines within the newspaper industry. The angle of theses studies, however, has been directed toward understanding allocation of company resources concerning various types of news and information items that at the end of the line constitute the daily product of a paper. The implications of a paradigm shift concerning media economics became quite obvious by using the same kind of methodology under auspices of various scenarios of prospective development of Internet services, of multimedia packaging and new systems of distribution within consumer mass markets on the local and regional level.

This paper, thus, tries to reconstruct the ways by which one enters a process of complete re-consideration of traditional media-based market analysis and is forced to opt for a new kind of methodology. One option, among a number of others, will be presented.[2]

This, hence, is a methodological study interested in the upcoming process of change that is challenging traditional media (cf. Zerdick et al. 1999). The analysis is

---

[1] This is an approach in contrast to rather large-scale types of study. Cf. European Commission DG XIII/E 1996.

[2] Hitherto, mostly, adaptations of newspapers on websites have been focused upon. This methodological option carries fundamental elements of newspaper economics into the new set-up (cf. Höflich 1998; Kamp 1998; Neuberger/Tonnemacher 1999; Sennewald 1998).

based on implications for local and regional daily print media to limit assumptions and empirical evidence in view of persistent strategies operating in particular markets. The pertinent case data and economic structural data backing our argument are those of the Federal Republic of Germany. Generalisation seems, nevertheless, justified because of structural homogeneity of the traditional economics of local and regional newspapers.[3]

The presentation is relying on arguments and results while detailed tabulations have been left out. Within expert circles the underlying processes and proportion of market performance of the newspaper industry are common knowledge, thus, this type of reference was considered negligible.

This paper is prospective in the sense of questioning the strategic concepts available at present within the newspaper industry of coping with upcoming multimedia and online products and services. The prospective horizon, therefore, is a situation in which, in fact, a majority of households of a given local and/or regional area have practical access to new digital services. This is actually not yet the case (Werle 1998). Development, however, in this direction is increasingly under way. The strategic challenge, therefore, cannot be overlooked.[4]

Perspectives of traditional economic assessment are major obstacles to the understanding of an innovative economic potential of a new type of regional and local communication industry. Following comparative results of a case study of traditional local and/or regional newspapers – based on data of the industry in Germany – it becomes evident that maintenance of orthodox patterns is largely influenced by vested company and shareholder interests. Strategies are not based on forward looking economic analysis. The upcoming economic perspectives of the multimedia era on the local and regional level is almost without exception considered rather a dream world (cf. McKnight/Bailey 1997). This study is based on the finding that an essential part of the strategic void within the newspaper world in view of a new technological future is the result of the belief that classical media economics is also serving as standard reference to understand the future of the communication industry. This analysis points to evidence that a new type of information economics will be replacing major areas of classical media economics and will be able to analyse processes by different and radically more realistic concepts of the future. The fundamental rift between these two approaches will be in the understanding of markets and of pricing mechanisms.

---

[3] Because of such structural homogeneity international case studies presented at the IFRA/WAN conferences, e.g. "Beyond the Printed Word" in Amsterdam in October 1999, were considered to be of paramount interest to participating newspapers and experts.

[4] The German Federation of Newspaper Publishers (BDZV) has started an initiative in September 1999 for a national digital online service for classified advertisements. Every member newspaper is invited to either become an active partner or to use the service infrastructure of this new endeavour.

1.2 Background of Analysis: The Traditional Business Strategy

Traditional methods of describing the economics of "classical" newspapers, i.e. local or regional papers, have established an analytical framework and a set of standard data procurement which reflect, mostly, institutional parameters of production, distribution and market success. To mention just a few of these standard parameters: cost per copy; income (distribution/advertising) per copy and per title; total cost per title per months for production and sales sectors (i.e. distribution, sales, printing, editorial work, administration) etc. During the last decade a lot of meticulous methodological work has been put into refining such parameters in order to arrive at insights into performance of newspapers on a more subtle and a more detailed level, including the editorial offices.

These data sets are a derivative of general company business administration under the prerogative of twin market competition of newspapers ("reader demand" and "advertising demand"). The element of analysis built into this particular methodology of data collection is bound by the following major perspectives:

- assessing competitive advantages in advertiser-/consumer-driven markets;
- productivity rationales based on inter-company comparisons to engage management in controlling practices.

The kind of aggregate data necessary for controlling performance of single titles in the newspaper industry are of rather simple nature, and there are only very few necessary for this purpose. Optimising performance of single titles within the newspaper industry, therefore, is much less complex, in terms of the economic aspects involved, than in a number of other product and/or service industries. Optimising in terms of quality of the product, however, often turns out to be much more complex than in other product areas. International comparative studies, hence, show that the standard procedure to optimise title performance in the newspaper industry follows a traditional hierarchy of instruments, mostly of this order (cf. Iglesias/Verdeja 1988):

(1) general cost controlling;

(2) redressing of advertising markets;

(3) changes in editorial leadership;

(4) rationalising measures based on technological advances in special sectors;

(5) product packaging measures;

(6) marketing and readership measures;

(7) content-related quality measures.

Measures involving the most complex nature of discussion and analysis obviously tend to follow at the lowest priority. We will see that this established scheme of economic reflection has a substantial bearing upon innovative priorities involved in view of upcoming multimedia challenges within the industry.

This study confronts traditional ways of economic strategy within the newspaper industry with challenges deriving from new ways of generating information, of information distribution, information processing and distribution and of new forms of information packaging and of new information services to be made available in the near future. Some of these services are already on the market (online databases, online news services etc.).

1.3 New Model for Economic Analysis in the Newspaper Sector: Scripts and Scenery

Only a very comprehensive synthesis of major ways of establishing comparative analytical insights into the newspaper industry will be given here. This look back is necessary to confront an established system of parameters and perspectives with changes through new technologies and possible impact through new methodological instruments.

The traditional working concepts of economic thinking in the newspaper industry is built on an "actors' model of communication". Participants of an established set and structure of communication, of routine forms and acts of communication in (local and/or regional) space and time follow a number of defined roles as citizens, as politicians, as journalists, and as established institutions of news providing, of news gathering and reporting. The benefit of these activities, again, is spread in a routine manner clearly streamlining supply and demand. Reliability in terms of the kinds of content, its packaging, the ways of handling, availability of the product are a major part of this specific "actors' model".

The governing rules in this model and its practice are clear, but not explicit. Actors follow a script; according to existing and implicit but established rules news is gathered and reported in line with existing scripts. An overwhelmingly large portion of these ruling scripts is of an underlying economic nature which, however, is not generally evident to the observer. The kind of scripts that define each role within the newspaper organisation are neatly interconnected. The nature of these scripts seems to establish the kind of product that is similar to the product of the day before except for the very "news" content of information, be it political or human information, service or advertisement. There are subscripts available for various elements of production. These, again, are interconnected and establish a rich system of routines, boundaries, responsibilities, controls, and measures to avoid risks. The economic, mostly invisible nature of these scripts, however, is based on a meticulously planned and experimentally fine-tuned system of input/output schemes of resources.

To give an example: the daily production of two pages of local news for town A can only be handled by one person in charge of content production if there is a guaranteed script working underneath, guaranteeing an input of prefabricated material of different communal sources demanding only minor alterations and editorial adaptations. Furthermore, there have to be similar scripts in action to guarantee responsible input by stringers, photographers etc. The economic nature of all these scripts governing the daily appearance of two pages of news for town A is set by three elements:

- a rigid spending limit (time and money);
- a clear definition of qualifying sources and the kind of information (production code);
- an allocation scheme (cues and priorities).

This type of economic modelling underlying the newspaper industry has historically been brought about by adopting industrial production processes after an initial long era of single product manufacturing operation that in most countries ended by the start of mass papers in big cities at the end of the 19th century. It is quite obvious, hence, that the subsequently emerging interconnected systems steering the world of media communication within the local and/or regional perimeter based on such "actors' models" were, of course, practically relying on complex processes of division of labour and its complex increase through advanced industrialisation. However, an even more complex system of integrating scripts of actors outside the company (news sources) has not been changed essentially during almost one hundred years of newspaper industry.

The newspaper as a local and regional actor is relying on established systems of production scripts that have turned into established general rules of the polity. Newspapers and their work are governed by a status of "detached observer", by "impartiality", by a "knowledge of important vs. unimportant" etc., to mention only a few of such abstractions of a polity consensus. However, these abstractions have their origin in nothing but the general sum of a complex system of staggered scripts and an underlying economy of production.

A generalisation of these scripts on their most abstract level serves a double purpose. This generalisation, on the one hand, enhances the coherence of the complex interplay of information scripts – meaning the general nature that they seem to carry – and their economic nature – meaning effectiveness within a company context. On the other hand, these generalisations support the interest of vested powers as news sources by providing an effective rationale of information distribution.

The inherent general tendency in society to turn one model of newspaper industry into a generalised model of information is quite obvious. Calling this established model an "actors' model of communication" on the local and regional level implies a "scenery". This "set" is permeated by the amount of positive and, first of all, economic advantages it delivers for all actors involved and by the established demand for the kind of product and services that the readership in these areas traditionally expects.

Based on these advantages this model and its hidden economics even proved to be able to successfully survive the era of multi-channel competition on the regional and local level (e.g. competition through regional and local radio and TV). This model, however, is not qualified to take care of the advent of new challenges brought about by the era of multimedia technology. The fundaments of the reasoning in favour of the latter hypothesis are economical.

1.4 Basic Elements of Communication Change: From Actors to Net-Streams

The starting period of new digital and multimedia technologies already has an impact on "classical" newspapers. The energy of this impact will increase. First and main inroads of change are: classified advertising and service-oriented local information. Within these areas Internet-based services not only constitute competition but will provide such services on a fraction of production and distribution cost and based on extremely diminished overheads.

The potential use of Internet-services in terms of traditional newspaper functions will, however, go much further. An entire spectrum of news services on the local and regional level will, in the near future, fall under siege of new competition based on new and upcoming technologies. The market potential of this future competition, however, cannot be gauged relying on traditional "newspaper economics" and its underlying actors' model. A new type of economic analysis has to escape the "actors' model of communication" and to come closer to the new context and market reality brought about by multimedia and online technologies.

The essential difference is the open system aspect of the upcoming communication world on the local and regional level (as generally in the world). A multi-channel type of communication world turns into a world not relying on media for its standard communication in society but on universal access modes. There is no chance for actors anymore because there would be too many. The basic structural model is a universal net and potentially point-to-point communication of everybody with everybody. This may, at present, still sound a little utopian, it is, however, in this direction that current developments lead. It is not the media that provide information transfer, the fundamental change is based on the fact that the entire system relies on data streams that carry all or only a selected part of the existing universe of information.

It is on this background and on the magnitude of the change involved that a new type of economy has to be looked for. We have based our analysis on the concept of streams, i.e. total availability of information, and, furthermore, on information items as the core measuring particle for transactions, hence market activities.

Information streams will constitute unique markets and market value will be built on types of information items. Within a changing environment of information demand on the local and regional level – due to ongoing technological progress – this new system of parameters will, in the end, redefine levels of traditional consumer demand and of specialised information supply; the latter being, again, advertising but also developments surpassing present types of advertising.

Experimenting with preliminary methodological steps for this new approach offers chances to overcome traditional media framework for further analysis and, particularly, for strategic analyses within the newspaper industry. Preliminary results of such methodological pilot studies lead to a number of questions to be entered into strategic discussions:

- Why and how can traditional set-ups of "classical" local and regional newspapers still prevail in an environment of upcoming substantial technological and economic change?
- What factors will determine the dynamics of innovation in this market area under the influence of new information technologies?
- What are the essential theoretical differences between traditional media economics and new avenues of information economics?

1.5 Establishing a Stream-Based Economic Model of Communication on the Local and Regional Level

We shall demonstrate a number of succinct steps to show that due to modern Internet services and multimedia technologies a new fundament is at the stage of being implemented within the next years on which a different and modern model of communication on the local and regional level is going to be established. This model will rely on a fundamentally new type of economic framework with no pertinent reference anymore to the still reigning and established "actors' model of communication".

1.5.1 *Step 1:* The Information Stream Model

Up to now an advanced model of media-based information on the local and regional level was built on media channel competition. The new era will be based on net-built and net-interconnected types of communication models (cf. Bakos/

Brynjolfsson 1999; Economides 1996; Ludes 1997; Mc Knight/Bailey 1997). The effects of this structural difference are tremendous on the following grounds:

- Within media channel competition the goal of every competitor has to be mass audience. Due to standard newspaper and broadcasting economy there is, generally, only one viable approach: to bundle for all possible major demands of the mass audience. This, however, means to provide for inputs at enormously high costs per input item. A mass carrier concept is economically much less profitable than a special carrier concept.

- Information on demand has been technically and economically impossible within the channel competition economy. The existence of such demand, however, has led to a number of programme and content surrogates within broadcasting and TV formats as well as readership hotlines etc. within the newspaper industry.

- Total interactivity built into advanced net communication will completely change the kind and type of information coming from and going to various sources within a net and it will, necessarily, put a complete stop to the traditional script-based type of information production and its built-in information economy.

- The complete disconnection of data distribution from data representation out-distances any kind of traditionally limited production format, be it in the form of a newspaper, a radio or TV programme. This holds true even more so on two extreme grounds: (a) cost differences between one form of data representation and another tend to be nil, (b) a transfer into traditional formats (like radio, TV, and newspaper) will be possible at only marginal extra costs.

In order to take into account the revolutionary impact of this new model of communication in economic terms – while not re-engaging into the classical telecommunication economy of net distribution, net investment, and rating systems – we favour the introduction of the concept of information streams. Information streams require just three modi operandi:

- rules of net access;
- technical protocols;
- workable pricing models.

The only surprise to be expected – within our methodological case – is in the latter element of workable pricing models; the spectrum here is not only vast but, up to now, not at all fully elaborated. Just to give one example: a particular data stream can be used free of charge for one part of the public, it can have minimal charges for another segment, and maximum plus staggered charges for a special segment. Generally speaking, pricing might even envisage a particular and different price for every participant within a given net structure. Furthermore, this type of extreme differentiation can be technically handled fully software controlled and fully in accordance with differentiation of content data and/or data representation. Information streams, in this respect, represent an entire universe of data available even within a limited area of local and/or regional concern.

1.5.2 *Step 2:* Transparency Services of the Information Universe

Within the information stream economy the universe of available data is being made transparent through systems using various methods, constituting themselves as services of their own. So far the full range of such services has not been fully elaborated. Systematic presentation of data, however, becomes one of the standard qualities within this new type of communication model on the local and regional level.[5] And this quality constitutes an enormous economic advantage in comparison to media channel based information products. The introduction of databases at the majority of source points within the net, renders the total quality of available information onto a completely new level of user quality.

Information stream economy, thus, tends to introduce completely different parameters of competition due to the underlying net structure and the universal concepts of total availability, through the introduction of standard measures of comforts of usage. Databank retrieval as a general standard of all streams will be such an element. It will be accepted as ground level standard.

Starting from such ground level, new products might be produced that initiate a kind of demand to finance themselves profitably in the long run. The interesting point of comparison is that in view of the daily content of traditional newspapers not one single type of information prominently qualifies to be directly turned into such an offer.

1.5.3 *Step 3:* Sources to Turn into Active Elements

Whereas in the traditional multi-channel competitive environment of the actors' model of local and regional media the standard selection of sources of information is handled through "sets" and the processing of this information is taken care of through "scripts" within the new information stream economy sources become completely liberated. They are on the one hand sources but they also turn into new acting information providers. Each source will no longer be just marginally active because of ruling "sets" and "scripts" but will become fully involved in the universal process of information exchange. The advantages of this change are quite obvious. The economic effects are positive because of much more

---

[5] Advance Publication, the third largest publisher in the U.S.A., follows this strategy in the state of New Jersey by offering community groups free sites (up to nine pages) in a "community publishing plan" comprising the entire state of 8 million inhabitants.

options to focus on informing effects by, at the same time, maintaining similar costs. A possible disadvantage in comparison to the traditional media channel competition era is a loss in continuing public presence and a loss of influence on agenda setting in the traditional way.

However, based on other developments within the information stream economy, services will certainly be established to prioritise again particular sources. There will be competition, nevertheless, between such services because of the effect that particular sources will certainly set up such services to secure visibility within the information universe.

1.5.4 *Step 4:* Spreading Information Competence Outside Traditional Media Institutions

Within the channel-based competition of local and regional media the know how of information retrieval, information processing, and information production is a prerogative of specialised personnel being members of these institutions. Only particular sources have the means to provide for adequate personnel to balance this type of professional competence on the part of the media carriers.

Information stream economy, however, will clearly equalise this type of competence in the long run, just because of the necessary technical know-how required by the type of information technology and the surrounding change of climate vis-à-vis information handling in private households, in small firms, in schools etc. There will, henceforth, be a deterioration of salary levels within a number of institutions, including the traditional media, for all functions involving standard information processing of the "crafts"-type that for once had been the core element of journalism training.

The levelling of this personnel market will invoke chances for functional specialisation at a number of sources. Other institutions will build up competences of a professional nature for purposes of their proper information processing. This process constitutes a de facto unbundling of the information tradition of hitherto established media in the local and regional universe.

1.5.5 *Step 5:* Systems of Information-Building Processes

Although one can talk about a general universe of information available within an information stream economy and its net structures, the pattern of usage will in the long run, of course, establish systems and sub-systems of interconnected sources/content providers that cater for particular areas of demand. These clusters will form the kind of structure that will come closest to our understanding of traditional media in the local and regional context. However, it is quite obvious that theses clusters have no similarity to the type, ways and processes of traditional media. Foremost, there will be constant change within such clusters because they are totally demand-driven. In this respect, especially in view of the pertinent element of routine and continuity attached to format and packaging of traditional media, there will be no resemblance between the one and the other.

1.5.6 *Step 6:* The End of Traditional Information Intermediary Processes

The traditions of information production that we are used to, in a more sophisticated or in a more banal sense, will fade away or will follow suit in altered contexts. A standard press conference of a communal agency does not offer much economic or informative sense in the new era – the number of technical solutions of information exchange, of information packaging in such instances is almost unlimited in view of the kind of data collection and representation. A media intermediary does not make sense at all in an era of information stream economy. The service of commentary, judgement and background will be provided by a number of services, most of them outside standard media traditions.

New information services will necessarily be tested. Their economic viability has to be tested. Enriched reporting becomes possible using segments of moving image and audio signals.

To imagine what such services will look like and how they will operate is too far-fetched at the moment. However, such services will have no similarity with local and regional media that we know because of the fundamental differences in economic structures.

1.5.7 *Step 7:* Disconnecting Traditional Revenue Sources

The standard financial instruments of traditional newspapers are based on one single economic speciality. A large enough segment of the population has to be willing to pay for a tiny bit of information that it really considers useful, thus, having to accept a heap of printed pages – a large part of which they consider waste. This method of financing will end if people pay less or even nothing for exactly the kind of information that they are interested in without bothering about the waste part of the deal. There might still be some years to go in the traditional fashion. However, the information stream economy has already become visible in its major outlines.

The dwindling readership of newspapers leads to a sudden death because of the advertising industry's keen interest in minimum contacts per market. In the regional and local advertising industry within recent years a growing segment of mass market companies have left newspaper advertising, favouring direct mail instead. This is an indicator of flexibility involved in strategic thinking on the part of the advertising industry. The information stream economy will offer, first of all, largely disconnected and singular formula for advertising. The present status of advertising within the WWW is offering an initial impression of ways and tactics. Within a regional and local context this picture will turn out to become clearer soon because of the limited net structure as operating ground. Prospects of success in this area are great because of the broad spectrum of options and the easiness of market entry.

1.6 Questions of Media Innovation in a New Key

One of the inherent problems underlying the kind of questions that derive from a new understanding of information economy in the media sector is media innovation. The traditional understanding of media innovation has had a strong if not unique emphasis on innovations in technology followed by business adaptation. In terms of a new information stream-based economy this singular understanding will not hold true anymore. The new key of media innovation will much more directly rely on information demand and extra-institutional incentives for information usage. Unfortunately, it is exactly within this area that solid economic analysis is most underdeveloped.

Standard economic analysis in the newspaper industry is following a business administration framework of rather orthodox nature. Due to this approach an analysis based on information item cost and on stream analysis is virtually excluded. Information item cost analysis is taking care of advances in the set up and processes of net-based and technologically advanced information gathering, production and distribution in the local and regional area. Information stream economy on the local and regional level leads to a totally different overall communication set up and turns the traditional "actors' model" into something rather outdated. The main ingredients of this model are:

- every member and every institution within the community and/or region is a news producer of their own;
- every member and every institution within the community and/or region demands news and information services of various nature;
- the value of each item of information is not based on information hierarchies according to pre-established scripts and actors' roles but only on its stream value within the interconnected set.

Stream value of a news item is a price derivative based on the following major elements of appreciation: singularity, continuity, reliability, instant usefulness, prolonged usefulness etc. There exist subsets for further more detailed criteria.

On the background of the traditional model of local and regional communication symbolised by the classical newspaper, its economy and information model, the new type of information stream economy offers a provocative rift from established traditions because of these cornerstones of a newly evolving system:

- every participant in the system carries a chance of providing information of a high demand nature;

- the option of offering information of high demand can be tested directly, i.e. without the intermediary service of a specialised actor;

- production cycles turn down to an interval of zero;

- information can, for the first time, be effectively stored and retrieved, and will be accessible on a permanent basis;

- a multi-systematic, and basically infinite approach of information design is available and operational.

Obstacles against a revolutionary reform of the media-based communication processes on the local and regional level are based on two major aspects and constitute an intriguing process of structural resistance against technology adoption and economics reform:

- The actors of the "actors' model of communication" on the local and regional level have strong, vested interests to maintain the traditional model. On the one hand, there are large and recent investments, e.g. in printing facilities, on the part of the newspaper industry. On the other hand, during recent years the most powerful actors on the political level have enormously suffered from public dissatisfaction, voting abstentions etc., and fear is evident that these forms of hidden protest might turn into more effective ways based on new communication technologies.

- The advertising industry on the local and regional level is not interested in a sudden change of its communication world because of the existing ease of established routines and still available mass audiences. One of the standard fears is to reach out for the real individual because of the chances of direct response.

There exists an intricate fashion to avoid confrontation with the strategic challenges involved through vested interests that try to corroborate and maintain an established mode of information economy. This established type of information economy is basically a true reflection of the traditional media-based industry and its multi-channel concept of competition.

The inner reasoning of vested interests is, of course, very plausible in economic terms. The present rates of profits would, obviously, be gone through adoption of new communication models within the immediate future. Comparisons of traditional production systems and a new systems of information service on the local and regional level show very clearly the impact and pressure that is behind strategic decisions concerning the future of media based communication systems in this area.

1.7 Conclusion

This paper was looking at prospective economic data on the company and on the market level under auspices of traditional media economics and under those of an optional information stream economy.

It has been a limited analysis due to the nature of underlying models and due to its focus on media-based communication on the local and regional level. Given these limits, the study shows, nonetheless, a modern example of Bernoulli's hypothesis: The utility of present arrangements including a comparatively high profit margin for carrying on the traditional way in the near future, is considered much higher than the risk of changing over to a new type of economic understanding.

At present, the number of households hooked up to the new nets has not passed over 30 percent. Tied in with this is a broad consensus that the daily use of Internet services is still limited by present tariff structures and lack of general practice on the part of all household members. These arguments, of course, carry weight. They carry less weight, obviously, each further day.

The structure of change is also determined by moral hazard – in economic terms – on the part of the owners of newspapers; the singularly high rate of return in the business with no considerable risk even over long periods of time enforces a mentality to insure traditions.

Our conclusions point to the enormous increase of market-driven inter-dependence of media services and products in the area of digital distribution and of multimedia packaging. Part of the strategy of the traditional newspaper companies to maintain their market power, thus, depends on a crucial analysis of the particular interdependence of single services that constitute the essential product value within their markets. This paper offers instruments to establish empirical precision for this kind of strategic analysis.

1.8 References

Bakos, Y./E. Brynjolfsson. 1999. *Bundling Information Goods: Pricing, Profits and Efficiency.* Working Papers No. 199. Cambridge, Mass.: MIT Center for Coordination Science.

Carveth, R./J. Owers/A. Alexander. 1998. "The Economics of Online Media". In: A. Alexander/J. Owers/R. Carveth (eds.). *Media Economics: Theory and Practice.* 247-273.

Economides, N. 1996. "The Economics of Networks". *International Journal of Industrial Organization* 14/2. 12-35.

European Commission DG XIII/E (ed.). 1996. *Electronic Publishing. Strategische Entwicklungen für die Europäische Verlagsindustrie im Hinblick auf das Jahr 2000* [Report by Andersen Consulting – Thomas Baubin, Peter A. Bruck]. Brüssel/Luxemburg.

Höflich, J. R. 1998. "http://www.zeitung.de: Perspektiven der Online-Aktivitäten lokaler Tageszeitungen. Oder: Das Wagnis Internet und der Verlust des Lokalen?". *Publizistik* 2. 111-129.

Iglesias, F./S. Verdeja. 1988. *Marketing y gestion de periodicos*. Pamplona.

Kamp, H.-Chr. 1998. "Zukunft Online? Zur Nutzung von Print- und Online-Tageszeitungen im Vergleich". In: I. Neverla (ed.). *Das Netz-Medium: Kommunikationswissenschaftliche Aspekte eines Mediums in Entwicklung*. Opladen/Wiesbaden. 277-298.

Ludes, P./A. Werner (ed.) 1997. *Multimedia-Kommunikation*. Opladen/Wiesbaden.

Ludwig, J. 1997. "Zur Ökonomie des Internet". In: K. Beck/G. Vowe (eds.). *Computernetze – ein Medium öffentlicher Kommunikation?* Berlin. 203-224.

McKnight, L., J. Bailey (eds.). 1997. *Internet Economy*. Cambridge.

Neuberger, Chr./J. Tonnemacher (eds.). 1999. *Online – Die Zukunft der Zeitung?* Opladen/Wiesbaden.

Sennewald, N. 1998. *Massenmedien im Internet: Zur Marktentwicklung in der Pressebranche*. Wiesbaden.

Werle, R. 1998. "High Tech – Low Use: Probleme der Marktentwicklung bei Multimedia". In: M. Mai/K. Neumann-Braun (eds.). *Von den 'Neuen Medien' zu Multimedia*. Baden-Baden. 58-74.

Zerdick, A. et al. 1999. *Die Internet-Ökonomie: Strategien für die digitale Wirtschaft* [European Communication Council Report]. Berlin/Heidelberg.

2 Electronic Books. Re-Inventing the Wheel in the Multimedia Sector?
Guiseppe Vitiello, Italy / France

2.1 Introduction

Endless effort and no result at all is well-illustrated by the English expression "re-inventing the wheel". For fear of re-inventing the wheel no researcher would repeat an operation or a process that has already been performed by other researchers having worked in the same field. Re-inventing the wheel is inherently banned from the artistic domain in which originality is a key aesthetic criterion to assess the quality of a literary or artistic work. In the Renaissance, the notion of invention was crucial for building up the artistic canon. Four centuries later, Rimbaud, the well-known French poet, synthesised this attitude with the celebrated motto "Il faut être absolument moderne".

Yet, not a few important discoveries have been the result of processes and procedures that can be named in no other way than re-inventing the wheel. At the basis of progress in science is often the repetition of experiments and tests that underpin a previous theory. Galilei critically reviewed all experiences and "scientific" trials made by his predecessors before coming to radically different conclusions.

Re-inventing the wheel is a widespread practice, far beyond expectations. Wheel producers, among many other actors, do it constantly. Charles Goodyear vulcanised rubber in the first half of the 19th century and obtained his first patent on this invention in 1844. To re-invent the (rubber) wheel has been one of those human achievements that have changed the course of history. After all, the way one disposes wheels, with four tyres arranged in a rectangle or two tyres in a single line is essential to determine, among other things, whether the body on top of the wheels is a Ferrari or a motorbike.

At the core of the publishing business is a constant re-invention of the wheel. Every year hundreds of thousands of titles are published, more or less different from the others and from previous ones. Nevertheless, nobody would blame a publisher for printing the nth edition of a classical work by Shakespeare, Balzac, or Tolstoi. Such works are eternal and published in millions of copies, reprinted as many times as possible, in hard cover, paperback, illustrated editions, with new introductions and bodies of notes or in elegant *de luxe*-editions in a limited number of copies. After all, every publisher, even obscure experimental publishers, live in the hope of unveiling a talented writer to the world, and in publishing terms, to raise the work written by the unknown genius from the status of undiscovered golden vein to that of a bestseller.

In the early Nineties conventional publishers – i.e. those publishers whose area of activity is essentially the print medium – started to being aware of the formidable pressure of information and communication providers and their possible role of competitors. A dominant opinion was heralding the end of the book and the advent of the new time of the electronic production and distribution of content. European publishers are jeopardising the opportunities offered by ICT by being largely unaware that time is ripe to convert themselves from the print to the electronic paradigm. Their long historical background is no longer an asset to survive in the electronic environment. Several reports, issued in particular by the European Union, strongly stigmatised publishers' attitude: they were accused of lacking vision and dynamism, of sticking to their well-established relation with authors and readers and of relying blindly to their traditional skills based on ownership on content (cf. European Commission DG XIII/E 1993).

There was some truth in these accusations, although critics themselves overstated or gave a misleading picture of the impact of ICT on the publishing business. That was the time of the spectacular growth of the CD-ROM market with bibliographic databases, encyclopaedias and dictionaries taking the leading role and the rest of the content expecting to booming likewise. CD-ROMs were deemed to be the ideal carrier for the content industry for they allowed for large storing capacities, quick searching possibilities, and easy downloading of data.

Such predictions, in fact, failed to become true. The curb of the CD-ROM growth escalated and then had a smooth falling down. Their ephemeral success was not to be premonitory either to the decline of the leading role of traditional print products in the knowledge economy or to a rapid replacement of paper-based products with electronic devices or to the shift from a single medium to a multimedia environment. If a new era of publishing was definitely blooming, no book murderer was yet looming at the horizon of conventional publishing industry, as such reports seemed to prospect.

2.2 Forecast 2000 and Consumers' Patterns

How optimistic the views were that animated the early Nineties' research in the field of electronic publishing can be gauged by the estimations of the market share of electronic publishing in the publishing business for the year 2000, as they resulted from several reports that enjoyed a relatively wide attention in the professional environment. In an influential report issued in 1993, the potential range of electronic publishing in the book segment was estimated 8-18 percent, with the STM (scientific, technical and medical) sector taking the lion's share with an estimated 20–30 percent of the overall publishing business. Legal and children's literature would be no less affected with a potential range of 15–25 percent. Estimations also assigned to educational material a market share of 10–20 percent (cf. European Commission DG XIII/E 1993). At the end of 1997, however, another study of the European Commission readjusted these figures towards less optimistic (but more realistic) targets. The market share estimation for electronic publishing by 2000 was reduced to 5 percent of the overall publishing market for the book segment (instead of 8–10 percent); STM publications would score 15 percent (instead of 20–30 percent) and education marked the lowest range (10 percent) of the previous estimation (10–20 percent) (cf. European Commission 1997).

Table 1: Market potential (potential range for the Year 2000) – Estimation 1992 and 1997

Segment	Potential range (Estimation 1992)	Potential range (Estimation 1997)
Books	8–18 percent	5–15 percent
Magazines	20–30 percent	5 percent
Newspaper	5–15 percent	
Corporate	5–10 percent	
TOTAL	6.5–15 percent	5 percent

Such (gu)estimations were indeed flawed with technological determinism and with the implicit assumption that content and ICT industries would inevitably converge into a broad techno-media industry. This philosophy was largely derived from the evidence of the many mergers and alliances between telecommunication, audio-visual and media industries. Horizontal and vertical alliances between the "convergent" industries were (and still are) making the headlines of newspapers and television.

Another weak point of these reports was that they overlooked the publishing business as a value chain involving information originators, producers and brokers before the content is made available to the users. Users themselves were totally disregarded and a long tradition of analysis on cultural practices was carelessly dismissed. According to the reports, the publishers' task in the electronic environment was solely that of a packager: to bundle texts, images and sounds in a single solution. The idea underpinning this concept was that publishers should not re-invent one, but three wheels, and set together audio, visual and text publishing. Users' behaviour was grossly simplified in so far as their sudden shift from mono- to multimedia patterns of reception seemed to be natural and solely driven by the new multimedia offer. The habit of, and the need for, a sequential textual way of communication was not even taken into consideration; the eventual acceptance by the large audience of the hypertextual structure of communication did not leave room for doubt.

In fact, this shift from a sequential to a hypertextual pattern of reception is far from being so natural as it appears from the above mentioned investigations. A Council of Europe study, elaborated in 1997, examined the reactions of the so-called "heavy readers", i.e. people who read from five to six books a month or even more, to the new media. In this study, the natural propensity of heavy readers to recognise CD-ROMs or the Internet as a reliable replacement for books was seriously re-questioned (cf. Council of Europe 1998).

Heavy readers are an interesting category to take into consideration, both for their social background (highly educated, high profile readers), their attitude to use content for professional purposes and their strong purchasing power. They show an open and unbiased approach to the new media with well-formed expectations and a strong curiosity for novelties. In the above-mentioned study, heavy readers recognise the following advantages in new media:

- immediate utility (for study and research);
- extensive range of content and interconnectedness;
- better and faster access (in relation to books) and good retrieval of information;
- active participation of users.

Together with that the investigation also found out serious limits to the acceptance of new media by heavy readers. New media are difficult to access and use. Unlike the book they have to be accessed through a computer device that, apart from cost problems, is a barrier to direct access to content. They maintain a high level of uncertainty for what concerns support and the hardware necessary to be able to read increasingly sophisticated software requiring enhanced memory. The material becomes rapidly obsolete and needs to be replaced. The present products lack appeal and the most shared sensation in accessing the Internet is one of being lost. All these factors are serious hindrances to the acceptance of new media by heavy readers that are, first of all, professional readers for who time and money variables are closely related.

In addition to that, the most interesting results of the investigation proved to be in the analysis of the cognitive and psychological processes linked with the reception of new media. Heavy readers claimed that, in spite of their sequential form of presentation, books lend themselves well to a hypertext form of consumption with "zapped" reading making the reader free to jump from one section to another of the text. Therefore, to the often-claimed freedom to navigate in the hypertext, heavy readers responded that, on the contrary, the user of a hypertext is more or less obliged to follow pre-set, pre-ordained paths. Conversely, while dealing with books, the reader decides which path of analysis and thought to follow. In other words, CD-ROMs and hypertexts create compulsory paths based on a rigid logical structure.

New advances in the field of publishing give evidence that there is no discontinuity between conventional and electronic publishing and that the emergence of new actors has stimulated the re-qualification of traditional publishers. The first have opened new avenues in the electronic book trade and the second gradually are catching up, thus making the most of the electronic environment. Just as libraries, publishing houses and bookshops have integrated into their organisational structure the electronic component by applying the "single-source/multiple-media publishing" pattern, i.e. publishing or distributing the same information source on different media such as paper, disk, CD-ROM, online, etc. The process of re-qualification which is still in course has not been easy but the dominance of the sequential structure communication in the knowledge economy remains uncontested.

This opinion seems to be confirmed by what may be considered the four major trends for publishing business in the new electronic environment: Internet bookshop, the rocket e-book, publishing on the Net, and print-on-demand. We shall mention the first three trends shortly and shall focus our description on print-on-demand.

2.3   Current Trends in the Electronic Publishing Business

2.3.1   Internet Bookshops

It is impossible to speak of Internet bookshops without mentioning the *Amazon.com*-phenomenon and the way in which this company has revolutionised bookselling. With an offer of over three million titles, *Amazon.com* achieves the surprising performance of having a net loss of 124.5 million dollars in 1998 with sales increased by 31.3 percent and yet remaining the darling of the stock market. The whole inventory of the English speaking publishing world is available on computer screen. For thousands of titles there are lists of contents, blurbs and even extracts from reviews. Books can be easily ordered and paid for by credit card. Moreover, the electronic layout is user-friendly and the offer contains the majority of titles people are looking for.

Amazon.com fulfilled a real need of the reader who felt frustrated by the limited offer present in physical bookshops. Another interesting feature of *Amazon.com*, and not its least recipe for success, lies in the large discounts it can offer in relation to ordinary bookshops (up to 40 percent). The fact of having the ultimate bookshop on the Net, with millions of titles in many languages, is definitely a significant advance in book distribution, ever since the weakest link of the book chain.

Book sale on the Internet is a widespread phenomenon with national applications or horizontal alliances between national operators. *Amazon.com* is outflanked by an ever-growing number of actors, but its stockholders have relentlessly invested in its innovative scheme and have not lost confidence in its future. The issue at stake in the sale of books on the Internet is whether *Amazon.com* will be able to reach the break-even point and balance the losses. The future of traditional bookshops is definitely to develop customer-tailored services online for their local customers.

2.3.2 Publishing on the Net

As long as no copyright law is enforced in the electronic environment, publishing on the Internet is still considered adventurous. Many electronic publishing houses are tooled up to operate on the Net with electronic catalogues, automatic downloading of texts, electronic invoices and payments through credit cards. Nevertheless, the absence of a regulatory framework permitting a stable environment for electronic commerce makes publishing on the Net a potential rather than a real business.

Nevertheless, two years ago the headlines of newspapers were announcing the successful launch of the *Encyclopædia Britannica* on the Net. When the news spread out that thirty-two volumes were eventually available online, ten millions visitors (!) per day rushed to visit the website. What is revolutionary is not the fact that the "Rolls Royce of knowledge" is online – this has already been the case for years with an online subscription of $5 per month, but the fact that this version is available for free and that the income derives totally from electronic advertisement.

By doing that, *Encyclopædia Britannica* has inaugurated a system of content distribution that is close to the ways in which, on the one hand, broadcasting programmes are channelled and, on the other hand, telephone companies are now making new customers. The revenues of private televisions are directly proportional to the income derived from advertisement schemes. Likewise, a number of telephone companies in some countries like Italy attract new customers by practising a system of tariff closely linked with the time made available for short advertisement messages. In the *Encyclopædia Britannica* initiative one has to applaud the principle that a body of knowledge, so far extremely expensive for ordinary budgets, is made available for free; nevertheless, its implication for the model of content transmission on the Internet raises more questions than it provides solutions.

Until now, the Internet pattern of communication has been a many-to-many model, where the supplier profusely transfers information to a great number of different users and neither the supplier, nor the broker, nor the user are much in control of the actual communication process. In the new pattern of communication inaugurated by *Encyclopædia Britannica*, there may be a possibility of a budding model of concentration of content in the hands of a few information providers able to distribute attractive content and being remunerated by advertisement agencies.

In this case, the model applied to the Internet would be that of a many-to-one-to-many pattern of control in which the broker acts as an intermediary between the original supplier of information and the user. Distributing the *Encyclopædia Britannica* becomes no different enterprise than channelling *Dallas* or searching on the *Yahoo!*-website. If in the case of *Britannica* the supplier has enough strength to act as broker, in other situations information originators should rely on brokers that would have the control of the market. The implications for a democratic access to content are enormous. But after all, *Britannica* has only treaded in the footsteps of *Microsoft*, which made the *Encarta Encyclopaedia* accessible at a low price, or even for free in promotional packages, to those purchasing *Microsoft* programmes.

2.3.3 The Rocket E-Book

The rocket e-book has the ambition of being the exact replication of books in electronic form. You open them as books; you turn over the pages by scrolling the text. You can make notes in the margins, find specific passages instantly, set bookmarks, underline text and change font size and orientation. It comes equipped with a backlight that lets the reader adjust the intensity, so that the e-book can be read everywhere. Moreover, you can earmark the passage you love by using electronic marks or electronic ink. And last but definitely not least, the rocket e-book may hold up to 40,000 pages of text and graphics in the palm of one's hand.

The launch of the rocket e-book permits to reduce room allocated for shelving books and to facilitate the portability of content and therefore responds to one of the major needs expressed by heavy readers. Moreover, it permits name search through the automatic creation of name indexes.

The ability of the rocket e-book of breaching into the market is linked with its capacity to download texts available on the Internet or to be bought within the rocket library. Its enormous memory capacities allow for the storing of texts that would otherwise require tenth of meters of a normal bookshelf. To this end, an alliance has been created between the *Nuvomedia*, producer of the rocket e-book, and the electronic branch of the major bookshop chain *Barnes & Noble*. A crucial drawback is that texts are solely available from *Barnes & Noble* and from some information providers like *AOL*. The possibility of downloading texts directly from the online offer of a publisher is, for the moment, excluded.

2.3.4 Print-on-Demand

The fourth innovative model is print-on-demand. Print-on-demand is an innovative new printing system based on digital technology that allows the printing of limited print runs at affordable prices. In traditional offset technology printing 100 copies may be almost as expensive as printing 1,000. Therefore, to achieve economies of scale and to make an edition commercially viable, the number of copies publishers must order is very often far beyond market needs. Print-on-demand, however, overthrows this principle. For, apart from fixed pre-mastering costs, every copy of the book costs the same. Print-on-demand is hence a convenient approach for print run up to approximately 500 copies, depending on the printing facilities available on national markets. For higher print runs traditional offset printing is more economical. Print-on-demand is therefore a solution for small print runs previously discouraged or prevented because of the high costs of offset printing and is ideal for cultural, non-commercial publications (cf. Council of Europe 1999).

Technologically, the process is easy to describe: the input is digital content in form of a disk or a formatted file. The output is a book. This simple process, however, provides a successful answer to the numerous barriers book professionals encounter in their work. In Eastern Europe these are: lack of capital, insufficient bookshop network, small language audience, bad distribution systems. In Western Europe: high costs for small print runs, the return of unsold copies from bookshops, increased fast sales due to tremendous overheads. Print-on-demand offers a technical solution that allows the printing of a book *where* and *when* it is needed. In the organisational discourse, this is to shift from a "just in case"- to a "just in time"-production process. In terms of freedom of publishing this is to magnify pluralistic expression beyond language barriers and commercial constraints. The current, cumbersome system of distribution and delivering will appear as what it is – a fossil in the new technological era.

Small and medium enterprises have paved the way for the application of this technology in Sweden, Italy, France, Russia. It would be false, however, to assume that print-on-demand is promoted exclusively by out of the mainstream actors in search of a new book trade continent. In Hungary a prime mover in print-on-demand is *Wolters Kluwer*, a publishing giant with a 3-billion-$-turnover, whose prospected merging with *Elsevier*, another giant, was abandoned after the objections of monopoly made by the European Commission. In the United Kingdom, the United States, and Germany print-on-demand publishers are mainly major wholesalers and distributors.

Print-on-demand is indeed a start-up business with a brilliant future. Umberto Eco and Nicholas Negroponte accustomed us to the idea that the third print revolution is at the door. At the beginning was the manuscript, then came movable types, and now the screen era. Robert Darnton and Roger Chartier, both historians, replied by describing the three reading revolutions, from the "volume" to the "screen" through to the "codex". In my opinion, print-on-demand may represent the third print revolution. The principle of economies of scale, which is embodied by the revolution of printed press in the 15th century, is overthrown by the principle of fixed cost. Simply put: in offset printing the first copy costs about 80 percent of the total print run, whereas the last copy costs hardly more than the paper it is printed on. With print-on-demand the print run has no influence on the unitary cost of the book, and the first page of the first book costs the same as the last of the last book.

Print-on-demand also provides an alternative way of content distribution. Content in an appropriate format may be sent to outlet points like traditional bookshops or other points of access where publications are made available through "digital printing *light*-equipment. Rather than for the production process, where print-on-demand is convenient up to a certain number of copies, the real future of print-on-demand is in the new model of distribution it contributes to create. The artificial borders set up by the distribution circuits, usually established at national level, become superfluous and may easily be overcome.

2.4 Cultural Policies on Electronic Publishing

In the Western world books have always been associated with the spread of knowledge and democracy, for the invention of printing has promoted the circulation of ideas and freedom of expression. And even today, and in spite of grand statements heralding the end of the book and the advent of electronic educational material, books are still the best weapons with which to conduct the fight against illiteracy.

There is practically no country in Europe whose cultural policy does not favour the production and spread of the written word. VAT reduction (down to 0-rates in some countries), fixed prices, subsidies for the publication of "quality" works, large acquisitions made by libraries and the like are some of the usual mechanisms by which book policies are made effective. This way the State guarantees the multiplicity and diversity of opinion and expression which strict conformity to market laws in the book trade would not be able to maintain. Many publishing houses are thus enabled to produce quality products that are not purely commercial.

There is dense literature concerning the measures devised by public powers in favour of book production and distribution.[1] What can be said is that even countries characterised by outright liberalism have devised such legal or policy machinery. What changes is the policy mix and the weight of the single actors within the general framework. Such measures, however, can broadly be divided into four categories:

- fiscal measures (reduced VAT rate, tax exemption for book import, etc.);
- mechanisms regulating demand (library lending rights, support to textbooks, fixed book price, massive acquisitions made by libraries, etc.);

---

[1] The Council of Europe and UNESCO have analysed book policies in several publications, cf. Baruch 1997; Garzon 1997; Rouet 1999.

- support to quality content (grants for publishing projects and for translations, etc.);
- support to publishing houses and bookselling firms (reduced postal charges, low rate loans, training, etc.).

Under the impact of ICT and, especially, in the light of the convergence between the telecommunication, audio-visual and media industry, these measures are being re-questioned. They are colliding, and sometimes clashing, with those devised for the audio-visual industry. In the perspective of the full liberalisation of services pleaded by the World Trade Organisation, they may even be considered protectionist. In order to keep them alive, therefore, governments have to re-think their approach and provide for new justifications. There are three possible options: a) to adapt them to the new technological environment; b) to develop a separate model for new activities, thus making a difference between regulations that are enforced in the printed framework and those developed within the electronic environment; c) to introduce new regulatory models in order to cover the whole range of existing and new services.

2.4.1 Policies Concerning Internet Bookshops

The development of Internet bookshops is the most serious threat to the system of retail price maintenance set up as a cornerstone of the book policy of several European countries (France, Spain, Portugal, etc.). Internet bookshops are in fact providing a fatal blow to independent bookshops, not so much because of their practically unlimited (virtual) offer of titles, but because such offer usually comes together with substantial reduction on the cover price of the book (up to 40 percent in the *Amazon.com* virtual bookshop). On the other hand, retail price maintenance has proved to be effective in protecting specialised and/or independent bookshops from the overwhelming dominance of large book retailers and supermarkets. They are irreplaceable outlets guaranteeing the diverse needs and reading practices of the public. Where there is no law on retail price maintenance, the decline of the number of bookshops has been indeed spectacular (60 percent in the last 20 years in Belgium, 30 percent in Sweden in the last 30 years), and the market share of book clubs has boomed (60 percent of the market in Sweden), resulting paradoxically in increased average book prices, especially for non-commercial publications.

The only policy that seems to be applicable in this domain is to maintain the retail price in the printed environment (a book on display is at any rate different from a virtual offer) and to devise support measures fostering the integration of bookshops into a system of electronic distribution based on on-demand technology. This package of measures should be culturally justified in order not to conflict with a possible move towards full liberalisation of services.

2.4.2   Policies Concerning Publishing on the Net

Publishing on the Net shakes traditional book policies from a different perspective. First of all, it must be clear that, as the investigation on heavy readers has shown, hypertext is a brilliant solution for knowledge transmitted in the form of encyclopaedia, dictionaries or bibliographic databases. These reference works are per excellence hypertexts and therefore their distribution online can only be enhanced by the speediness and the quality of information retrieval with cross-queries and the use of Boolean search tools. The system of transmission online seems to be less appropriate for that material whose sequential structure is inherent to its communication pattern. It is, indeed, less advisable to make works of fiction, literary prose, essays, and all other genres available on the screen where the linear form is an essential component of their communication format.

In terms of public policy on electronic publishing, however, this is irrelevant (after all, every publisher is free to decide how to distribute the content they produce). The case of *Encyclopædia Britannica* raises a different set of questions. When publishers distribute their content for free and generate income through advertisement, the natural trend of the market would be to create vast content aggregates having a publication attractive for advertisers as flag offer (like *Encyclopædia Britannica*). Charging the user for accessing the additional content on offer would then create the publishers' added value.

In the pattern just depicted a change of great importance is to be noticed. The initial model of distribution on the information highway is often described as intrinsically democratic for it does not imply any barrier between the information originator and the user. Instead, advertisement combined with publishing may lead to a highly selective communication pattern, with heavy pay tolls for those users willing to access content designed for limited audiences. The entry barriers publishers find in the distribution of "difficult" content in conventional publishing would be magnified in the globalised information market. What chances are offered to, let's say, Lithuanian or Moldavian publications to find their way onto the Net and being associated to best sold information packages? The most likely consequence is that content of a non-commercial nature or produced in a less diffused language would automatically be excluded from the mainstream of electronic publishing.

Hence, the need to set up policies concerning the development of cultural content on the Internet by using the traditional arguments justifying cultural intervention: removing entry barriers for new actors and finding remedies to market failure. In Canada, for instance, the fear of losing local and diverse identity in the face of dominant US cultural industries has facilitated the setting up of measures oriented at the production and distribution of Canadian content on the Net. New services and products are now circulating on the information highways with governmental support. They concern the development and the use of navigational systems in the national language(s), the creation of governmental web sites, and substantial grants given to heritage institutions and cultural agencies.

These measures, too, must now be justified against global agreements. After all, the free of charge availability of content such as the *Encyclopædia Britannica* – a kind of basic service – can only make millions of users happy. It must be kept in mind, however, that the generation of income through advertisement in electronic publishing is, in this case, the result of a quality offer based on a large amount of research, generally of non-commercial nature. This is a good argument against the controversial concept, very often endorsed by the European Union, that there is no difference between the realm of network industries (telecoms, cable, Internet) and the domain of content providers (broadcasters and publishers).

2.4.3 Hands-off Strategy for the Development of the Rocket E-Book

The rocket e-book has still to go through the ordeal of the market before becoming a well-spread devise. So far, its prospects are not clear. Firms producing the rocket e-book are tying up strategic alliances with Internet bookshops with a view to making electronic texts available downloaded in the rocket e-book. There is a double move, both vertical and horizontal. On the one hand, by acting as a ready-made outlet for content directly made available from the Net, rocket e-book manufacturers become information suppliers. On the other hand, by acquiring the rights for the distribution of the electronic copy of a text previously published in printed form, Internet bookshops become information brokers. The possibility for the rocket e-book of becoming a universal carrier, thus replacing or at least substantially complementing the traditional printed book, lies in its readiness to drop proprietary standards and to become a universal device. Any form of content should be accessed from any content originator. Like mobile phones, the rocket e-book becomes a "mobile" book, with the same portability as a book but no fixed, pre-set content. It can be filled up at electronic kiosks by electronic distributors and content providers; and even offered free of charge – as it happens today with mobile phones – to subscribers of electronic information packages.

If this is the future of the rocket e-book, with clients adopting hybrid practices and shifting from paper to the electronic book – just as they move today indistinctly from the fixed to the mobile telephone – interference of public powers will only be deleterious. Competition will rationalise current strategic alliances between rocket e-book producers and Internet bookshops for the benefit of users and will increase the penetration of rocket e-books among individual customers. If the product proves to be successful, a hands-off strategy on the side of public powers is the most appropriate means to guarantee a diverse content and cultural pluralism.

2.4.4 Policies Concerning Print-on-Demand

Print-on-demand should be the darling of policy-makers in the field of culture. It meets the needs of less diffused languages and alleviates the constraints of non-commercial content. It allows authors in these languages to have their works published at low cost. It permits academic publishing for local markets to be in existence. It breaks down national borders by diffusing literature beyond traditional distribution circuits, thus encouraging dialogue and intercultural exchanges and fostering freedom of opinion and pluralistic views. It may help foreign languages to penetrate the Anglo-Saxon market, one of the most self-sufficient in the world, where no more than 2 percent of all titles are translations. It may allow, for instance, Albanian, (or Armenian, or Georgian) writers to diffuse their works in Albanian (in Armenian, in Georgian) for the diaspora and to print them locally, where emigrants eventually settle down.

As yet, no significant changes have been undertaken by policy makers in this field. Lack of awareness and, sometimes, of imagination may well account for that but are no satisfactory explanations. A good reason is inherent to the creative role of publishers that consists not only in manufacturing a book, but also in selecting titles and setting up a convincing publishing policy out of them. In other words, in situations where public grants are at stake the pre-selective role of publishers is a guarantee that the publication has already been the object of an intellectual assessment and risk evaluation.

In fact, print-on-demand does not exclude the selective function of publishers but solicits public powers to re-design book policies insofar as support to textbooks, massive acquisitions made by libraries and grants for publishing projects are concerned. Instead of providing direct support to the print of research or literary publications, public powers should shift towards the support of marketing schemes elaborated by publishers in the form of just-in-time delivering of the desired material. Titles being awarded for public support should be given the chance to reach their direct customers (universities, libraries, and individuals) through networks beyond distribution barriers. Apart from cuts to public spending, this move initiated by public powers would be a decisive boost for the re-design of a more rational (electronic) publishing chain.

Of course, print-on-demand does not exhaust the range of measures that public powers may put in place in the field of electronic publishing. They may facilitate the progressive re-shuffle of the relative positions of book actors and the optimisation of functional relations among book actors. By setting up well-funded programmes for re-qualification of book professionals, public powers may help in re-orienting them towards new tasks and functions. Whatever the strategy, however, all measures should be oriented at guaranteeing creativity and cultural diversity, access to content and participation by all groups of population in a sound and open-to-all European information society.

2.5 References

Baruch, Olivier. 1997. "The Book Sector and the State: Relationships in Change". In: Council of Europe (ed). *Legislation for the Book World. Proceedings of the International Conference and Workshop (Warsaw, 13-15 November 1996)*. Strasbourg. 227-247.

Council of Europe (ed.). 1998. *Heavy Readers: Their Practices and Reaction to Multimedia.* Strasbourg.

Council of Europe (ed.). 1999. *Freedom to Publish (on Demand) our Cultural Diversity.* Strasbourg.

European Commission (ed.). 1997. *Electronic Publishing in Europe: Competitiveness, Employment and Skills.* [Report by IDATE, France]. Brussels.

European Commission DG XIII/E (ed.). 1993. *New Opportunities for Publishers in the Information Services Market. Main Report.* Brussels/Luxembourg: ECSC-EED-EAEC.

Garzon, Alvaro. 1997. *A Guide for Users in the Field.* Paris: UNESCO.

Rouet, François. 1999. *VAT and Book Policy: Impacts and Issues.* Strasbourg: Council of Europe.

3 Changing Business Models of Online Content Services and their Implications for Multimedia
Robert G. Picard, USA / Finland

3.1 Introduction

This paper focuses on the business models for online content services and how they have changed during the past two decades as technology changes and audience demand have affected operations. It explores how the current business models emerged, how new developments are affecting those models, and the implications of the changes to producers of multimedia and other content producers.

The paper explores the bases and problems of four major failed business models, how they evolved into the primary models existing today, and the prospects for the future. Such business models are important to understand the context and strategies of the major online content service providers and how producers of content are and hope to be able to co-ordinate or integrate their operations to gain benefits from the strengths and opportunities provided by these operators. Major operators are necessary for the development of independent producers of multimedia and other content because they provide access to the distribution systems and entry points that are necessary for commercially viable operations.

The paper discusses the underlying economics of these systems, how and why current business models are employed, and how independent producers are crucial to the success of the new business models.

3.2 Influences on Demand for Information and Communication Technology

To begin, it is useful to undertake a broad perspective regarding the nature of modern electronic communication capabilities. Although the term "revolution" is often applied to contemporary developments in information and communications technology (ICT), the technologies should not be confused as being part of a content revolution. The revolution is in software, equipment and infrastructure and in their capabilities for presentation and dissemination but not in the substance of the content itself.

This is an important element in understanding the nature of demand for the products and services associated with new technology because it comes to the core of the question of who will use the technology, for what purposes, and at what price.

If one looks past all the marketing and excitement surrounding the technologies, new ICT based technologies cannot revolutionise content because they provide no real new communications capabilities. They are not affecting communications in such fundamental ways as did the arrival of the printing press, telegraph and telephone, photography and motion pictures, and broadcasting, which provided the abilities to move text, sound, and images with or without terrestrial lines.

If one carefully considers the combination of computers and tele–communications, it becomes clear that the convergence is not producing any revolutionary change in communication. Rather, its primary effect is increasing the speed and flexibility of communication. The most revolutionary aspect of the technology is that it creates new economies of scope and integration that change the economics of content distribution. New technologies permit the combination and integration of the other existing means of communications and allow readers/viewers/listeners more control and choice.

This is not designed to give the impression that these developments are unimportant. The combination of existing content modes creates new methods of presenting content, the new technologies provide flexibility of use, and they shift control over communications. All of these factors provide significant advantages to users. And where there are advantages, there are consumers willing to spend time and money.

However, the demand for the products and services providing these advantages must be understood as a part of and an extension of demand for existing content products and services. That demand is within those who communicate and receive communications using existing means. New methods of accessing, using, and combining that content must increase value to these users and help simplify their search for and access to the content.

It is ignorance or misunderstanding of this essential demand element that has made it so difficult for so many firms to find ways to profitably exploit the potential of the new ICT technologies and associated products and services. Many believe the rhetoric that new and unique products and services are being created that will alter the behaviour of individuals and transform society. In reality, these products and services are just creating faster, easier, and more flexible means for consumers to do what they are already doing.

Coming from the business perspective, it is important to understand that this demand and a variety of forces from within and outside the ICT industry must be harnessed in order to create sustainable products or services.

The success or failure of new communications technology is not dependent upon whether it is innovative, useful, or desirable but rather on questions of whether it can find a means of obtaining and maintaining sufficient usage and turnover so that it is not rejected by users, entrepreneurs, or financiers (Picard 1998).

The competing interests of a variety of factors play significant roles in the process, and the area in which their interests converge is relatively small (cf. Figure 1). When those interests do converge or can be accommodated, the likelihood of success of a new application or technology increases. When all interests intersect the degree of risk is low, but for each interest that diverges the risk of failure increases.

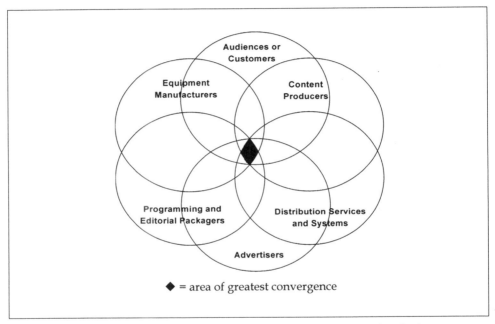

Figure 1: Convergence of Interests in Communication Technologies

This means that the technologies and their associated applications will succeed only if the market believes that they create value that is absent today and that they are able to fulfil needs of businesses and consumers that cannot be fulfilled by alternatives that are less costly or disruptive to current business operations and consumer behaviour.

It is exactly this problem that makes many sectors of the ICT industries so risky and has forced entrepreneurs and those with high-risk venture capital to fund most new communications technologies and applications. This has been especially true for developments involving Internet and multimedia, where limited patience for results has caused the rapid movement of financial resources from certain products or services to others that are perceived as having more potential to create sufficient demand to make the product or service viable.

There is no single formula for creating a successful arrangement within the interests, and different firms and technologies seek different models for transferring the potential of technologies into successful business enterprises.

Basic to these, however, is the issue of creation of content that is of interest to users. Advances in the development of interactive and multimedia technologies are increasing the number of producers and the availability of content and are forcing traditional information and publishing industries to develop a new understanding of their roles in creating, processing and storing content (cf. European Commission DG X 1998).

The development of electronic publishing, which is often based on content generated through traditional publishing, has created a growing sector of economic and pushed traditional content providers to enhance their competitive-ness and survivability in the face of new entrants from audio-visual, multimedia and other sectors (cf. European Commission DG XIII/E 1996; European Commission DG XIII/E 1997).

European publishing industries have some advantages over multimedia and other new content producers because they are part of mature industries that do not face the developmental and resource problems of European communications firms in audiovisual production, multimedia, information technologies and tele-communications (European Commission DG III 1999, and European Commission DG X 1998).

As publishers and multimedia producers have moved online in Europe and worldwide, a variety of different arrangements to co-ordinate the needs of content producers, content organisers, technology providers, and the others have been attempted. If one looks at the arrangements carefully and combines issues of investment and operational capital, there are clear models that have been adopted across sectors of the ICT industries at different times. In this paper I will focus on the models that have been employed in the online content sector.

3.3 The Nature of Business Models

The term "business model" is often confused with that of "strategy", such as company strategies, product strategies, general marketing strategies, or pricing strategies. Strategies are the means employed by firms to meet their goals (Grieve Smith 1990; Karlöf 1989). A business model is much more fundamental, however. Business models are understood and created by stepping back from the business activity itself to look at its bases and the underlying characteristics that make commerce in the product or service possible. A business model involves the conception of how the business operates, its underlying foundations, and the exchange of activities and financial flows upon which it can be successful.

Business models have been described as the architecture for the product, service, and information flows, including a description of the various business activities and their roles. They include a description of the potential benefits for the various business actors and the sources of revenues (Timmers 1998). In terms of modern communications, business models need to account for the vital resources of production and distribution technologies, content creation or acquisition, and recovery of costs for creating, assembling and presenting the content.

A business model then embraces the concept of the value chain, that is, the value that is added to a product or service in each step of its acquisition, transformation, management, marketing and sales, and distribution. The value chain concept for products and services is now well established in business literature in which it was widely embraced after its exploration by Porter (1985). This value chain concept is particularly important in understanding market behaviour because it places the emphasis on the value created for the *customer* who ultimately makes consumption decisions.

The issues of value chains and value added are especially salient in European settings where value-added taxes rather than sales taxes are the traditional methods used by government to raise revenue. As a result, many European firms have an advantage in identifying and comprehending the elements of value chains over firms in nations and regions where value-added taxes are not present. Despite that advantage, however, even many European businessmen and women are unable to identify the value added by their activities. This is problematic because if one cannot articulate that value, one cannot properly manage and market a product or service.

Understanding the business model under which a firm or product operates or will operate is especially important when new products or services are developed or the industry in which one operates is in a state of significant change. As the environment in which a firm or industry changes, the factors that support a business model change simultaneously. As a result, business models that may once have been successful may become less successful and be abandoned. Business models that seem appropriate for new products or services may not produce the support and structures necessary as the business milieu changes and may then be altered or abandoned in favour of other models.

Some individuals make the mistake of assuming that failed or abandoned business models can never again be successful. This is not always the case if the conditions in which they failed are no longer present or resistance to some elements disappears. A situation may then arise in which such a model may be reintroduced successfully for the same or a different product or service.

3.4   Business Models of Online Content Services

We may now focus on the business models of the major online content service providers, those firms that provide users access to content of interest including news, information and entertainment, leisure activity, and other materials.

In this discussion we are not focusing on Internet service providers but rather those firms who make their business in organising materials and providing access to content. This includes firms such as *AOL.com (America Online), Yahoo!® MSN™, Netscape Netcenter™, Excite.com*SM, *CompuServe.com, digitalcity.com* and scores of similar organisers. In terms of usage, these content organisers provide the most visited sites on the World Wide Web. If one considers the top 10 websites receiving most visitors in March-April 1998, all but one – Microsoft's home site – are general online content organisers.

Table 1: Most Accessed Websites in 1998*

Rank	Online Content Site
1	yahoo.com
2	netscape.com
3	aol.com
4	microsoft.com
5	excite.com
6	geocities.com
7	infoseek.com
8	lycos.com
9	msn.com
10	altavista.digital.com

* counting unique visitors, 12 years and older

Source: *Relevant Knowledge*, March-April 1998

These sites no longer provide mere organisation of and access to information sources but are broad service portals that provide free e-mail, messaging services, voice mail, user customisation, online shopping, notification services, software downloads, chat lines, and access to a wide variety of online communities and content.

It is useful to consider the evolution of general online content providers and the various business models that have been used during their history in attempts to recoup investments in development and operations. One can divide the history of online content service providers into periods coinciding with four abandoned business models, a model in current use, and an emerging model evolving from the existing model.

These models can be labelled: (1) the videotext model; (2) the paid Internet model; (3) the free web model; (4) the ad push model; (5) the portals and personal portals model; (6) the digital portal model.

Each was made possible by particular developments in technology, had different financial bases, and produced different results, as outlined in Table 3. The importance of the technological developments that made the services possible cannot be diminished because these were very often the results of significant financial investments involving agencies and firms other than the content services whose purposes were not always similar.

Table 2: Business Models for Online Content Services

	made possible by	financial bases	result
Videotext	change in production, method of print, media and cable systems	secondary use of available material for a small fee or a promotion for newspaper	audience rejected
Paid Internet	US military-industrial complex investments	telephony style pay-for-use	audience rejected
Free Web	European nuclear science community investments	cost paid by content providers	audience accepted; commercial content providers and content organisers rejected
Internet /Web Ad Push	additional use of internet service subscription lists and ad placement on web pages	direct mail style advertiser payment and advertisement in specialty publications	audience services, and many advertisers have rejected
Portals and Personal Portals	changes in server and software capabilities	newspaper and magazine style advertiser payment	audience and advertisers are accepting
Digital Portals	digitalisation of audio and video media and telecommunication improvements	cable and satellite service subscriptions; pay-per-view	audiences, advertisers, content providers and online services indicate support

3.5   Four Failed or Abandoned Business Models

3.5.1   Videotext

Videotext indicates the initial attempts to use television screens as a means of conveying text-based content to a wide audience. Efforts to create videotext as a commercially viable activity emerged in the 1970s and were led primarily by newspaper companies in North America.

The impetus for creating this new content service resulted from newspapers' change to ICT for photo-typesetting. Because the new processes associated with the technology captured keystrokes, it was now possible to reuse or easily alter content prepared for the newspaper for use in a videotext operation. Supporting this use was the development of cable television systems that could be used for easy and inexpensive distribution of the content. The concept of videotext was particularly attractive because it would allow publishers to update materials and convey breaking news during the times between printed newspaper editions.

Because most of the infrastructure, content creation and formatting costs were already covered by revenue from the newspaper operations, the financial costs of this secondary use and distribution of the content were relatively low. This permitted publishers to offer videotext at a low price or to provide it free as promotional costs for the newspaper itself. Some television channels produced similar content offerings, reusing material prepared for magazine and newspaper program listings and marketing efforts in what became the initial forms of text TV that are now more common in Europe than in North America.

Although the producers of videotext had strong technological development and cost advantages in producing and distributing the material, the consumers – either as audiences receiving it free or purchasers of the service – were generally uninterested. When tested or implemented, use among the public was relatively low and only occasional. It became difficult for many producers to justify even their relatively low expenditures given the performance in the marketplace. As a result, most content providers abandoned the videotext model. It still exists in a few locations where acceptance was higher or where it plays a larger role in the marketing strategies of the content producers.

3.5.2   Paid Internet

When videotext did not produce results desirable to content providers, they did not abandon the prospect of additional use of existing materials. Rather, they began to seek methods through which costs could be recovered from individual users and perhaps generate profits.

This possibility would only be viable with a pre-existing infrastructure, and it soon became clear that the Internet was the most attractive alternative for distribution of the materials.

The existence of the Internet and the software required for its operation had been funded by the United States government as a communications system between the Pentagon, military contractors, and scientists working on military projects at universities in the late 1960s. The U.S. Department of Defense Advanced Research Projects Agency (ARPA) created the *ARPAnet* – the first nationwide computer communications network (Cringely 1992) – to communicate and co-ordinate activities because research, development, and manufacturing were well-distributed in different geographic locations. By the 1970s the system had spawned the Internet to link sites not engaged in military projects, primarily universities.

The existence of this system and its potential for commercial use were used to change the system to allow wider use and access. Content producers discovered by the last half of the 1980s that they could make their materials accessible through the Internet and charge a fee for access to the content. Many of the producers who originally considered videotext and numerous others moved to provide material to users in this manner. Consumers would pay either flat fees for access or pay per actual usage typically charged against a pre-existing account set up for the customer.

The market, however, did not look so kindly on the development. General audiences who could wait a few hours to receive the information in print did not embrace the idea of paying more to get information just a bit earlier and were often unhappy with the complicated processes required to access the information. The greatest market success was not for general information providers but for specialised data providers such as those creating and distributing financial information. As a result, general content providers soon began abandoning the model based on providing content through the Internet and recovering the costs from audiences.

3.5.3 Free Web

Although general content providers rejected the paid Internet model, the benefits of Internet distribution remained attractive. But the complicated processes that audiences disliked and difficulties in displaying content still remained.

These problems were removed by the creation of the World Wide Web and associated software and browsers. These technological developments were not the result of the content or ICT industry investing to solve the problem, but also came from governmental investments. In this case, the technology resulted from efforts by the European nuclear science community to improve its ability to convey data, graphic displays, and other materials to researchers throughout Europe and the world.

Work for the European Centre for Nuclear Research in Geneva and in particular the efforts of Tim Berners-Lee, UK, produced the World Wide Web and introduced it as a workable alternative by the early 1990s (Pavlik, 1996). The widespread distribution of browsers in standard software packages for new computers, as well as their availability in retail stores, rapidly made the Web the primary online use of general consumers.

With this infrastructure and acceptance in place, content providers began moving to the Web. Many new types of content providers began moving rapidly onto the Web, exponentially expanding material available each year. These materials were generally provided free of charge as promotional materials for commercial firms or as special interest materials provided by individuals or organisations.

Media and other content providers soon grasped the utility of the Web in providing advantages for distribution and creating a system in which individuals could access materials they produced. Some began operations to reuse existing materials again – as they had under the videotext model – but this time with the advantages of true graphic capabilities. Other firms developed means to organise materials in a way that reduced the frustrations of users seeking content.

Users of content found this arrangement quite workable. Because the material was free of charge the lack of cost made use the equivalent of obtaining material from free television or radio and this appealed to consumers. The model of operation, however, did not provide means for commercial firms to recover costs for providing material or organising content from the users so they soon rejected the model as not workable for their firms.

3.5.4 Internet / Web Ad Push

The desire to find a mechanism to find a non-user revenue stream led some content providers, Internet service providers, and content organisers to attempt to use lists of subscribers and users, combined with demographic, lifestyle, and other profile information obtained through registration, as a means of attracting advertising that could be targeted to specific users. In other cases they attempted to find advertisers for products and services related to web pages on which particular content was organised.

In both cases, the firms "pushed" advertising toward audiences that would be most interested in the products or services offered.

The first process made secondary use of subscription lists and information and created an advertising system based on direct mail models in marketing through printed materials, the second process followed a system based on advertising in specialty publications.

Although the model created a revenue stream to support operations, audiences were unhappy with content and service providers who used such systems because they saw it as an intrusion on their mailboxes or felt they were confronted with too many advertisements when they reached sites. Internet service providers and content organisers did not want advertisers not associated with them to use their system.

Many advertisers saw negatives in the intrusiveness of individually directed ads. In addition, they questioned the effectiveness of the model particularly because it was difficult to measure the effectiveness of mere exposure to the limited advertising messages on many sites.

3.6   The Current and Emerging Business Model

3.6.1   Portals and Personal Portals

Content organisers needing to gain the advantage of the advertising revenue stream but also to control advertising exposure soon moved to the current business model based on portals. In this system users of web browsers are brought to an organising interface and advertisements. As users move to information of interest, additional or related advertising appears. As providers have attempted to differentiate themselves and increase satisfaction with portals, personalisation of portals has developed.

The current revenue model is based on newspaper- and magazine-style advertising in which readers are brought into contact with advertisers' messages while making other use of the pages. In most portals only a single ad appears on each page and because of its limited size it is designed to "pull" or attract users to click through the ad to gain additional information from the advertiser.

The current model is attractive to many of the major players because user resistance is not strong and a regular advertising stream is being produced. A variety of arrangements are found in payment terms for portal web advertising, the most common being based on page views, flat rates, or click throughs. Where advertisers engaging in direct electronic commerce are involved, revenue splits, transaction fees, and customer acquisition fees becoming common payment terms as well.

For its improvement on other models, however, the current model is still not producing profit for portal operators. The major players are expending large amounts of risk capital obtained through stock offerings in hopes of creating strong brands that can survive until the current technology and applications are surpassed by improvements that create a new environment and hopefully profitable business model.

This strategy is based on the fact that portals create value by organising access to content in a way that creates a brand for the portal that attracts returning users.

A side effect of this strategy is that portals rarely create significant content. Content creation is expensive and difficult so portal operators primarily make deals with those who have content to enhance its availability to the wide audience of users that the portals create or to create additional revenue streams or brand identification for the content creators.

3.6.2 Digital Portals

The current hope for portal providers, backed by significant investments and new competition from telecommunication firms, is the development of multi-purpose digital portals. Digital portals, which are not yet widely available because bandwidth and compression technologies are still being improved and installed in many locations, allow the combination of the aspects of current content portals with digitalisation of video and audio.

Under this concept video and audio can be pulled over telecommunications lines and accessed using Internet-based applications. It is believed that fully digital portals provide the best means for searching, selecting, purchasing, and using content by organising access to the available materials in a commercially viable manner. A user of such a system could utilise a portal to view broadcast channels world-wide, to obtain pay-per-view services, to view potential non-broadcast channels, to search video clip archives, to use a variety of multimedia materials, to seek additional information about the content, to chat with others while viewing a programme, and to determine the language in which the content is received.

The ability to recoup costs by obtaining revenue not only from an advertising stream but also from users through pay-for-view and premium services makes this model attractive to a variety of players. The major content organisers in operation today are hoping to use this new environment and business model to capitalise on strong online portal brands created during operations under the current model. The telecommunication firms planning to enter the market are hoping to capitalise on the brand recognition they already have as well. This new environment is attractive because it will require only limited new technology investments for content providers and organisers. Similarly the consumer costs for acquiring new hardware and software will be relatively limited. For consumers, such digital portals represent a kind of kiosk or corner store for online communication. They can use the new portals to access online news, to view magazines, to make purchases of goods, to rent video or audio products they do not wish to own, to use education and training materials, to obtain cultural materials, and to play games.

3.7 Implications of Online Content Organisers to Multimedia Producers

The improvements of portals and the new business model that may support them are important to producers of content, especially multimedia producers. The emerging model would seem to provide significant opportunities for independent producers. When multimedia, audio-visual, and audio producers make materials available in the new model they can do so at no cost (sponsored by the company or advertisers), through pay-for-use, or as direct sales.

Digital portals become especially important in this regard in that they reduce marketing costs for the producer. The largest potential audiences and highest number of users for multimedia products are more likely to be gained by portal click-through than by independent click-through or information or product seeking in retail stores. Online use can provide samples of the materials even if full access is not provided.

Portal operators will be willing to deal with independent producers because their own brands are enhanced by availability and the operators will not have to bear the cost and risk of content production. The same types of relationships that exist between portal content organisers and content providers today are likely to be transferred to multimedia providers. When multimedia providers offer materials for a fee, it is likely that digital portal operators will use similar types of transaction or customer-based fee arrangements that are now becoming common in e-commerce.

The new digital portal environment further reduces the previous advantages of company size in content production by reducing traditionally needed marketing, sales, warehousing, and distribution operations. It increases the competitiveness of independent and small producers by providing easier access to the marketing and distribution systems needed by providing direct sales mechanisms, by reducing the need for warehousing, and by reducing the number of physical copies of products that must be produced for retail sales.

As portals continue to develop the need for video, audio, multimedia, and related materials by their operators will induce them to work directly with producers to gain access to materials. Multimedia producers, then, can benefit significantly from the further development of online content services. To do so, however, they need to become increasingly familiar with the business practices and strategies of the existing and emerging content organisers and to begin developing alliances to provide that material and gain access to portals from which new customers and financing will emerge.

3.8   References

Cringely, R. 1993. *Accidental Empires: How the Boys of Silicon Valley Make their Millions, Battle Foreign Competition, and Still Can't Get a Date*. New York.

European Commission DG III (ed.). 1999. *Competitiveness of the European Union Publishing Industries* [Report by Media Group, Turku School of Economics and Business Administration, Finland]. Brussels.

European Commission DG XIII/E (ed.). 1997. *The Content Challenge: Electronic Publishing and the New Content Industries* [Report by Techno-Z FH Forschung & Entwicklung, Austria]. Brussels.

European Commission DG X (ed.). 1998. *The Digital Age: European Audiovisual Policy*. Brussels.

European Commission DG XIII/E (ed.). 1997. *Electronic Publishing in Europe: Competitiveness, Employment and Skills* [Report by IDATE, France]. Brussels.

European Commission DG XIII/E (ed.) 1996. *Electronic Publishing: Strategic Developments for the European Publishing Industry Towards the Year 2000 (Executive Summary)* [Report by Andersen Consulting – T. Baubin, P. A. Bruck]. Brussels/Luxembourg.

Grieve Smith, J. 1990. *Business Strategy*. Cambridge, Mass.

Karlöf, B. 1989. *Business Strategy: A Guide to Concepts and Models*. London.

Pavlik, J. 1996. *New Media and the Information Superhighway*. Boston.

Picard, R. 1998. "Interacting Forces in the Development of Communication Technologies: Business Interests and New Media Products and Services". *European Media Management Review* 1. 16-22.

Porter, M. 1985. *Competitive Advantage*. New York.

Relevant Knowledge. *Web Access, March-April 1998 period*.

Timmers, P. 1998. "Business Models for Electronic Markets". *Electronic Markets* 8/2. 3-8.

4 Electronic Publishing for New Markets. Marketing Paths for the Content Industry in Europe
Peter A. Bruck, Austria

4.1 Introduction

Put into perspective and considering close to 200 years of industrial development electronic publishing (EP) is a very new and diverse business for publishers. It is also a market which publishers do not have to themselves, but where they have to face stiff competition from other industries such as telecom operators, video game producers, broadcasters or even consulting services.

In addition, EP is reshaping marketing and branding strategies for existing print publishing products. EP serves to draw more attention to them and is, for instance, used as give-away. EP then develops into commercially interesting add-ons and becomes part of new products and services.

Marketing electronic products requires that publishers are willing to find new ways, means and models to service their customers. Especially, online electronic publishing has entirely different kinds of economics and the business logics are far from being clear.

In this paper I would like to review some of the arguments which Thomas Baubin and I have made together with our research teams in 1996 when we published our study for the European Commission on the Future of Electronic Publishing (cf. European Commission DG XIII/E 1996). I want to set out what marketing approaches have proven to be failures and how to get around the most obvious pitfalls. I would also like to analyse marketing and demand generation strategies for electronic publishing products.

4.2 Dual Market Structure of the Publishing Industry

As most scholars of the traditional print media know, the marketing issues faced by publishers are fundamentally different from those of other industries. Publishers face the task to serve more than one master. They have two prime customer markets: their readers and their advertisers. They have to reach and satisfy these two groups of customers at the same time, despite the fact that the interests of these two groups hardly coincide and are often in considerable conflict.

The dual market orientation of the publishing industry shapes their marketing strategies and the interest divergence and conflicts between the two customer groups also effect the emerging EP market.

In some segments of the publishing industry the market situation is further complicated by the fact that publishing does not only serve the private interests negotiated between buyers and sellers, but that this exchange has important public functions in terms of the diffusion of information, the increase in knowledge and public awareness. Our modern systems of democratic governance are based on this function and state supports for newspapers or book publishing are in many European countries central to the financial viability of the publishing industries.

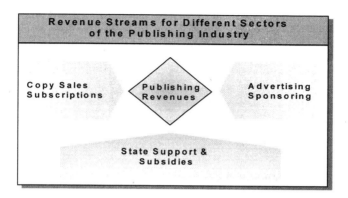

Figure 1: Revenue Streams for Different Sectors of the Publishing Industry

Thus, three sources for publishing revenues have traditionally supported publishing in Europe: copy sales and subscriptions, advertising and sponsoring, and state support and subsidies.

It is obvious that marketing considerations and models have to take into account the different market structure for publishing and the difference in revenue sources and streams for various sectors of the publishing industry. Publishers' income varies considerably in the different sectors. The survival of an independent, national book publishing industry in some European countries such as Austria depends almost entirely on the support and subsidies given by federal ("Länder") levels of the state to companies and individual projects.

State support structures newspaper publishing to a lesser degree. In some European countries, however, state intervention and sizable grants are the order of the day. Distribution subsidies in Finland or Sweden skyrocketed between 1971 and 1991 and led to a considerable restructuring of the marketing models employed by the industry. Other direct support includes, for example, the compensation payments for economically weak papers of the Dutch press or the repayment for telecommunications costs by the French government for newspapers in that country.

Indirect support includes reductions in value added tax rates for newspaper sales which are reduced to nil in almost half of the EU countries and similar, but more modest VAT reductions for advertising revenues in countries like the

Netherlands or Greece. Considerable indirect support is given to the marketing of periodicals by reduced postal rates or lowered tariffs for paper imports. Both are common in most of the EU member states.

On the other hand, there are broad sectors of publishing where the revenues come entirely from reader markets. High-end STM publishing or popular fiction books get their revenues solely from subscriptions or from copy sales.

Thirdly, free sheets or many business and some consumer publications depend entirely on advertising income and are part of focused marketing strategies by advertising customers to get the attention of readers when these are not primarily interested to pay attention and expend money.

The structure of revenue generation differs also within sectors and also across EU member states. Such is the case in daily newspaper publishing where some tabloid papers generate up to 80 percent of their revenues from copy sales, while German home town papers can count on making 60 to 70 percent of their income from advertising sales. Party or former party newspapers in Italy or Austria, on the other hand, plan their business on the basis of more than 50 percent of their revenues coming from state support and payments.

It is only reasonable to expect that such differing income streams also effect the interest, ability and willingness of publishers to get into EP and that in some cases publishers might think that their is no economic or other benefit to be gained from EP. They will remain, however, a more and more dwindling minority.

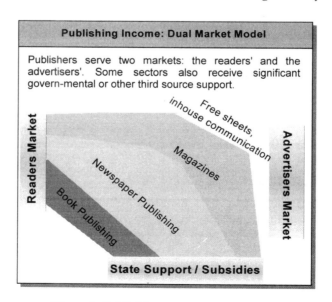

Figure 2: Publishing Income: Dual Market

Marketing, marketing objectives and strategies in publishing are governed by the dual market structure and the triple source of income. The digitisation of publishing dissolves the hitherto quite stable boundaries and some of the key challenges lie in the way how to successfully tap into more than one revenue source, a difficulty well known to all online publishers trying to sell ads.

In this paper we concern ourselves with the restructuring of markets and marketing in the dual market structure leaving the discussion of the third source to others.

4.3 Electronic Publishing: A New Market is Developing

4.3.1 EP: Mature versus Immature Business Propositions

The markets for electronic publishing and, particularly, for online publishing in Europe are still in their start-up phase. Mature technologies exist on the production as well as customer end, but the market development is still in its infancy. CD-ROM publishing became a sizeable market only in 1992/93. Online services or internet publishing have gained a broader public and customer base since 1995, but they are offered largely as free services and the paid contents are far off.

The EP markets are thus low in revenues and many players are still testing the "waters". As the examples of the *Microsoft Network* or *e-World* demonstrate, marketing problems abound also in more developed markets and even the biggest players face considerable set-backs and losses.

There are no proven marketing models for EP available anywhere. It will still take quite some time to have such models developed. But the current experience already provides the opportunity to develop new skills and some new revenue sources now.

A common understanding is developing that it does not suffice to transpose one medium into the other. Moving from newspapers into EP raises hard questions such as format of content, use of multimedia features and layout. Most users of online services do not accept a one-to-one electronic copy of the traditional print (TP) product, and CD-ROM publishing as well as online services need to find and develop their own message forms, new content formats and new types of professional content creation, e.g. journalistic practices and styles.

4.3.2 Trial Stages

Publishers have to provide added value to customers with the new electronic, digital products. Developing such features requires new skills and the knowledge of how to use the electronic means most effectively.

It is obvious that publishers find it hard to leave the world of print and paper behind and realise the new opportunities. Their scepticism, however, opens the door for other players to enter these emerging markets and set the *de facto* product standards and shape customer expectations. Thus, it is not surprising that some of the most successful online publishing sites are run by broadcasters such as CNN, BBC or ORF and not by publishers coming from the print and paper business of mass media.

But one can find many conflicting examples. The experience of the *Washington Post* since 1996 shows that many users being online want to see their electronic newspaper in a format familiar to them, no matter how many advantages an entirely new and interactive electronic version might offer. They are interested in seeing what *The Washington Post* has put on Page One. They want to find their "Style"-section, etc. Such modelling the EP product on form and features of print product does not only comply with some customer expectations, but it also makes considerable economic sense when done in a way that does not require excessive person-hours and does not interfere with the online structure.

Another challenge is content. The question is: What are the EP users actually interested in? Online papers like the *Rhein Zeitung*, a regional newspaper in Germany, changed the content in the EP version and put a higher focus, for example, on computer-related issues. The online version tries to inform about fewer events but cover these in greater depth. In addition, the *Rhein Zeitung Online* is updated quite frequently.

Getting into electronic publishing, publishers use different strategies. Newspaper and magazine publishers going online follow three quite different paths:

- INTERNET-BASED SERVICES. More and more newspapers and magazines operate worldwide online services on the Internet (or have them under development) – today all of them on the World Wide Web with some continuing database pushing. All but a few offer their online content for free, with some basic revenue coming from online services. Usually the online ventures are financed by the publisher's risk capital, they are considered as "strategic investments". Many of these Internet newspaper services are new and remain experimental. Only few are charging for access (e.g., *San Jose Mercury News*).

- AFFILIATION WITH COMMERCIAL ONLINE SERVICES. Many newspapers operate online services on the platforms of commercial online services such as *America Online* (AOL), *CompuServe, Prodigy, MSN,* and *AOL/Bertelsmann.* Charging for access in this category is also quite different. Some of these newspaper services are included in the subscription price of the online service (e.g. *Chicago Online*, a service of the *Chicago Tribune*, has no access fee beyond the normal AOL charges). Some others are charging an extra access fee, e.g., *Atlanta Online*, a service of the *Atlanta Constitution Journal* available on *Prodigy*).

- DIAL-UP BBS. Users dial in to a local phone number via modem to connect to a bulletin board system. Most BBSs are locally orientated services, offering local content and chat/discussion forums. Between 1996 and 1998, 39 newspapers operated BBS systems, most of them – 37 – were located in the US.

Despite the recency of the EP developments – most European newspaper and magazine publishers would not have considered going online as little as five years ago – the issues of the emerging markets are becoming quite clear:

Table 1: Issues in Electronic Publishing in Europe

Motivation	• gain experience (testing & trails) • innovative character (reaching young reader) • occupying market segment
Profit / Break Even	• no profit now • some hope for a break even after 2-3 years • calculation of costs varies greatly
Source of Revenue	• publisher's risk capital • access fees, subscriptions • advertising • cross media
Costs / Investment Volume	• around 100,000 Euro per year (very much depending on the status of the EP product within the underlying product/market matrix)
Size of Online-Team	• around 3-15 persons (mostly full time): online journalists, web designers, technical staff, etc.
Content	• using the same information sources as for print products • in the beginning still strongly orientated on print product • slow development of community and commerce features
Cannibalisation?	• No. EP is, on the contrary, strengthening the print product and developing separate product identity.

4.3.3   A Market without Profit

EP revenues are up in the offline business, but profits are quite uncertain. In the online market, publishers have not found ways to earn money. Most of the newspapers started going online in order to gain experience or for specific marketing purposes like proving an innovative character.

Currently only few online ventures can generate revenues at all, let alone profits, and those who do, such as the *Playboy* site, do it due to their particular adult content and to its well-known branding. *Playboy* and similar sites have to be considered a special case and cannot be compared easily to other EP products.

Publishers offering EP products on commercial online services can count on getting between 10 percent to 30 percent of the connect fee based on how much time is spent by members in their online areas. But the 90 percent of newspaper publishers being online do so without much expectation to earn money from their readers. A broadly accepted billing system is still missing in Europe.

As a consequence, online advertising and sponsorships are currently the key sources of revenues. But earning money out of selling links or classified ads is quite a hard business. Advertisers migrate to a few sites where traffic is particularly high and these are often not those provided by traditional publishers, but include service sites or search engines.

In addition, some advertising customers are getting themselves into content provision spending millions of Euro on developing and maintaining their Web presence and see little reason why they should spend more money on advertising on someone else's site. In general, the efficiency of net advertising cannot be measured clearly enough and it is too early to talk about an efficient targeting or rate of return.

The value of a business without near term profits is not obvious to most publishers. However, it should be understood that online electronic publishing has to do with both telecommunication and publishing. Achieving near term profitability as a new entrant into the telecommunication business is definitely very difficult if not impossible in the short run. All online businesses in the USA made this experience, some of them are not profitable to this day and it is reasonable to expect a large number of market actors not to survive in the mid term. The shareholder value to be created when entering the online business lies in the building up of a large and stable user community. Hence, the following reasons apply for a publisher who expects to generate longer term value at the expense of short term profitability:

- gaining experience in building a position in the online EP market;
- being in the market to capture (and hold) subscribers early;
- building new skills internally for online content management and development, community development and editing chat line operation, subscriber management, technical operations and software development;
- building an innovative image.

The New York Times started in 1996 to experimentally run a subscription model for their international online service. Within the US the New York Times could be accessed without being charged since it is supported by advertising (with some premium surcharged services, such as a personal news clipping agent and searchable archives). To access www.nytimes.com from outside the US subscription was required. International Internet users had to sign up for the service which offered 30 days free use before charges ensued. While initially offered at a 50 percent discount, the full-term price introduced was $35 per month. The newspaper repeatedly delayed to begin charging anyone, but people from around the world submitted their credit card numbers. Some of those intended subscribers were likely to drop out when asked to pay for the service offered.

While the number started off tiny, they exceeded the projections. *New York Times* did little marketing of the service outside the US. Plans were to begin soon by working with Internet service providers in other countries and placing ads in the *International Herald Tribune*.

4.3.4   EP Advertising: A Service Hard to Sell

While journalists might like to believe that advertisers use newspapers because of the quality of the news surrounding their ads, salespeople know advertisers use newspapers primarily as delivery vehicles. They look at market penetration in appropriate demographic and distribution areas and at the cost per thousand readers to be reached. If another medium can provide the same audience at lower cost, the advertiser is likely to go there.

Online advertising is the real wild card in generating revenues for EP. Currently online advertising is mostly "just" for getting as much experience as possible in the online world. The experiments are mainly testing the "pull" of online advertising, in other words the advertisers are testing how to get customers to "pull" product information from the Net. The technical features provide opportunities to meet some requirements of advertisers like stimulating awareness, motivating consumers or efficient targeting. In traditional advertising this has become more difficult, since consumers are increasingly ignoring traditional forms of advertising and they are scanning through the pages or jumping between TV-channels.

Most online advertising spending comes from advertisers' research and design budgets. Overall, advertisers have been slow to jump on the online bandwagon, devoting slightly less than 1 percent of their annual ad budgets to online ventures between 1996 and 1998, according to *Advertising Age*. The chart below demonstrates this relation in the UK. The estimated advertising spending shows a growth, but also that this figure is and will remain tiny compared to the spending on TV or for Papers.

P.A. Bruck / Electronic Publishing for New Markets

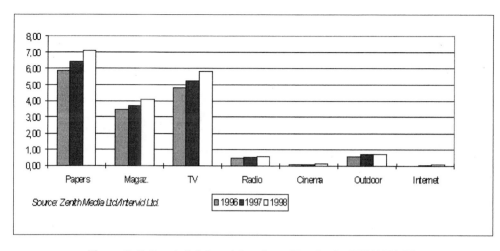

Figure 3: Estimated Advertising Spending in the UK (1996-98)

In a number of business sectors the use of online media has become a significant part of the marketing budgets. In the lead is the computer hardware and software sector where the Internet share of the total marketing budget exceeds 20 percent. Significant shares are also expended by the human resources industry, the financial services and the retail sector. In these, as well as in business and supply services the internet share is growing.

While the share of expenditures is not overwhelming, the growth rates are impressive. The retail non-hardware/software sector leads the industries to growth. The chart below shows the spending for advertising as a percentage of the total marketing budget.

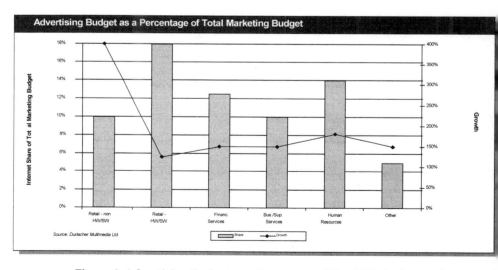

Figure 4: Advertising Budget as a Percentage of Total Marketing Budget

This research on shares and growth rates should add an optimistic tone to the tough business prospects of the EP business in the online area. Advertisers are spending money on their net presence and will do so in significantly increased manner over the next three to five years. For publishers the key challenge lies in their ability to bring these marketing budgets as advertising to their sites and services, rather then see themselves passed by new forms of direct marketing expenditures.

Publishers need to be aware that they command important assets to keep advertisers and show added value in the publicity game. As many advertisers are discovering that having an online presence on the Web is of little value if there are inadequate means to directing customers to those sites. Publishers have it in their hands to offer advertisers in their traditional products the publicity which will draw attention to the advertisers' online presence and get users to visit the site.

With less than a quarter of the total EU population capable of accessing Internet and commercial online services, the potential audience for any online advertiser is still limited in quantity. It is therefore not surprising that companies mainly in those sectors where customers are frequent and ready users of PC communications, move towards using networked media in their marketing. However, the penetration rates of the new information and communication technologies in businesses and households are climbing rapidly, with in some countries in Scandinavia already reaching over 35 percent and usage rates follow closely.

"Push" versus "pull" marketing

Electronic publishing is an entirely different carrier medium for advertising than traditional mass media. While it has been possible to avoid adverts in print from the very start of the commercial press, turning the page quickly was not possible in the electronic media until cable and satellites started to allow zapping or VCRs were outfitted with a fast forward option. Electronic publishing adds to these increased technological possibilities, freeing users from having pushed unwelcome messages their way and having their attention occupied by unsought material. Scanning over ads is increased by click away options.

In the publishing context the online media offer, however, also new possibilities for advertising, which can generate new marketing possibilities by strengthening the information function of advertising. Readers require product information about goods and services and online users can tailor the advertising they need and want to their requirements and liking.

EP offers the possibility of interactive advertising. Current market research testing online advertising found that users are accepting interactive ads as valuable source of product and service information. In addition, online advertising is also seen to be suggesting that the advertiser is on top of technological developments and new emerging markets.

Interactive advertising provides for more and customer-driven forms of information depth. But it also allows for a more "storytelling" and narrative mode to attract consumers and relate information to them. Given the features of interactive communications like e-mail, which can be integrated or attached to adverts, advertisers can combine the advantages of mass marketing with direct response advertising and on the spot sales.

The arguments for interactive online advertising can be summarized as follows: Taking the example of the World Wide Web as a form of electronic publishing medium, advertising online provides for updated information provision, better targeting, and an active consumer reaction, which can then be used to give more transparency about the entire exchange. The shift towards interactive online advertising meets the increasing information demand of consumers. Especially products requiring some explanation can profit from this. The key of successful online advertising is gaining the awareness and the motivation of the customers. In opposition to the traditional way, where advertisers are pushing the customers to get them informed about the qualities of a product, the interactive approach stimulates the interest of the customer who starts pulling the information from the advertiser.

Table 2: What Makes Advertising on the WWW Interesting?

Active Consumer Reaction	Updated Information
• reaching the customer in the "pulling", not in the traditional "pushing method" • it is like "Information-on-Demand" • reaching active consumers with high awareness and motivation	• unlimited amount of information • interactivity allows user to select what she/he is interested in • information can be kept updated very easily
Better Targeting	**Transparency in Using Advertising**
• addressing target groups more efficiently • lower targeting losses • addressing young people that are difficult to reach in traditional ways	• interactivity enables feedback analysis • more detailed information about user behaviour, e.g. number and / or duration

Using advertising successfully as the source of revenues enables the publisher to provide online content for free. This potentially generates more hits, i.e. the number of times that files are retrieved from a server, which in turn makes the site more interesting to advertisers. The issue emerges whether advertisers really want to reach those who they actually do reach. Here publishers who provide clear and good reader statistics for the EP products and services should see themselves in an advantage.

The revenue possibilities from EP advertising differ in a number of ways. Within publishing there is disagreement between publishers about that issue of who can benefit from this revenue source. Some say that advertising may be a meaningful revenue source only for large publishers, capable of attracting global or at least national advertisers. Local or regional advertisers, the key customers of most publishers in the print and newspaper business, remain interested in traditional publishing and only few are showing interest in online newspapers.

Not every business sector using advertising expects advantages from using online advertising to communicate product qualities to customers. Very successful are ads in the travel and holiday industry. The features of online advertising can be used here in an optimised fashion. Sectors to expect positive results from advertising online:

- Travel agents, tourist associations, hotels;
- providers of concerts and theatres;
- sports equipment manufacturers;
- home electronic distributors;
- media;
- mail order companies;
- political parties, associations and institutions.

4.3.5 Demand for New Skills

EP is a new medium and marketing it requires new skills. But the skill factor' goes beyond finding new strategies. It entails considerable reorientations in the knowledge and proficiencies in demand. New skills are demanded from those creating content, such as journalists or book authors, but also from staff serving online customers or from customers themselves. To develop an online service a publisher needs to have people who are professionally able to do the following things:

- MAINTAINING LARGE SETS OF INFORMATION: lists of URLs, phone numbers and e-mail addresses;
- WWW-AUTHORING: constructing useable hierarchies of online documents and understanding the principles of HTML;
- SEARCHING ONLINE ARCHIVES: composing concise sets of articles for users' reference, database authoring;
- FOLLOWING AND RESPONDING TO USERS' DISCUSSIONS: moderating chat lines, answering e-mails.

The requirements along the underlying value chain are listed in the chart below:

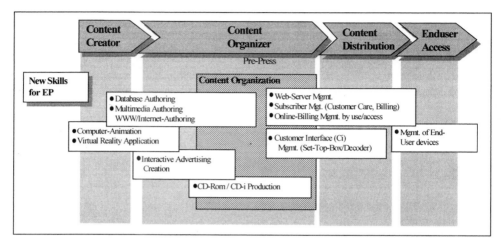

Figure 5: New Skills and Competencies Needed for EP Products

While journalists' skills suit many of the requirements of an online newspaper, a person's previous online experience is crucial in this EP environment. A smart person with good journalism experience can, of course, learn a lot about the online world in a fairly short amount of time, but there might be some differences between a person who has "lived online" and someone who has not. The same holds true for other staff involved in getting EP products and services to their customers.

Journalists training to write for print and paper and having little or no online experience often tend to think in terms of stories, news value, public service, and things that are good to read. These are the staples of success for a static and one-way medium. To this one has to add a thinking which revolves more about connections, content organisation, movement within and among sets of information, and communication among different people.

Thinking about an electronic information space requires conceptualising a place where people spend time informing and entertaining themselves, a place they return to again and again, rather than a product they receive, use and then quickly discard.

People who have not "lived online" do not seem to know this. They see a flat screen and tend to equate it with flat paper. Involving users and/or non-journalists with a strong user-interface background is crucial to marketing success. It forces to keep the online concept intuitive to the non-journalists who are the users. This also keeps the online project on a track which could introduce a combination of customised "information, communication, entertainment and transactions" and lead to some community.

Computer animation and Virtual Reality applications are likely not to be required for most of EP, but developments may lead to some demand over the next years. The *Chicago Tribune*, for example, re-launched its website and works with applications and plug-ins like Java, Shockwave and Real Audio. The *Chicago Tribune* website is on the way from EP to multimedia creation and addresses presently more the high end/power user, whereas the online version on AOL is more for online beginners or those who do not want to use sound or moving pictures online. The demand for multimedia-authored websites is rising and, thus, the next phase in EP marketing is developing.

The job assignments and production roles of journalists have changed over the last two decades with the introduction of IST systems and the computerization of writing, layout, pagination, typesetting, and plate production. Keeping a job in the publishing business over the next years means picking up some additional new media skills. Good candidates for a new media job in EP need to have sound experience and skills in traditional editing and reporting, combined with:

- experience in the online world and the ability to use the Internet as a research and communication tool;
- the ability to write HTML and create web pages;
- graphic design and layout skills; and
- versatility, such that they are prepared for the broad range of tasks they will be asked to perform in the new media environment.

In marketing terms, EP is at first seen by publishers as a good means to attract attention to their products, thus, to find new customers, but most importantly demonstrate willingness and ability to stay abreast with market developments.

While many are clear about the fact that their core business is still in the production of words amended and supported by still pictures, graphics and illustrations, most know that the new opportunities of EP can be most quickly and easily used in the marketing of the already existing products and services.

4.3.6 Why going online, ever?

EP is a new medium. Whilst media in the past have each been unique, EP means the integration of much that has gone on before. Newspapers have dominated the public media market till the 1920s to find their rivals in radio stations. The twenties and thirties as well as the forties have been the decades of radio, which was superseded in the fifties and sixties by television.

It is a truism of media history that no new medium has made any old one obsolete. But it is also correct that each old medium has been transformed by the new successful ones entering the market.

EP is unlike any of the other new media of the 20th century. It does not merely base itself on the exploitation of a new technological possibility. It does that undoubtedly by the force of digitisation and networking. But it also does more in bringing together publishing, broadcasting, computing and telecommunications, as the three extensions of EP products show:

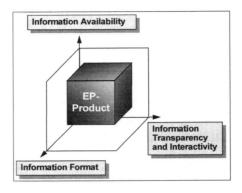

Figure 6: The Three Extensions of EP Products

Publishers should consider this integration the challenge and also the cause for getting involved with EP. A number of "push" and "pull" factors can be identified which might rank high in the marketing considerations of publishers:

"Push" factors

One of the key factors for publishers moving into EP is that print operations are getting more and more costly and that the industrial aspects of the publishing production increase their share of the overall cost of the operations. Prices for news print have been rising dramatically in all European countries over the past years, with some publishers having had to calculate double costs compared to two or three years ago.

Paper use and paper production also raise important environmental concerns and publishers associations across the continent have become very sensitive over the last decade to environmental issues. EP has the potential to free the publishing process from some of the resource constraints.

Production and environmental costs increase the prices consumers have to pay for publishing products. Already, there are many experts who maintain that key products like newspapers are too expensive and that the shrinking penetration rate and the decreases in reading times will force publishers to raise prices even further.

These factors are pushing publishers to consider EP a welcome solution to the crucial aspects of the outlined problems. EP can be seen as a marriage between dramatically lowering manufacturing costs through elimination of print and paper and tapping into an expanding consumer market which is less restricted than the ones hitherto aimed at.

"Pull" factors

While many publishers lead by those from the newspaper industry see themselves being pushed into going online because of industry-related economic and environmental factors, they are also being "pulled" into EP. Market forces attract them as online services and Internet are rapidly increasing in size and are creating an immense marketing glow and presence. Increasing signs that audiences are, at least to some extent, willing to pay to get certain information online and certain contents offline, pulls them. The users of the EP products, which are offering specific added value to special customer needs, pull them. As newspapers are traditional information brokers, there is an affinity between them and the new medium. This affinity is strengthened for newspaper as well as magazine publishers through the strengths they have developed in reader services and customer care over the last two decades.

Publishers are also "pulled" by the readers since EP products offer an added value. Exploiting the possible advantages of EP products, especially by combining text, picture, motion, sound with interactivity and creating a context to bring the information across most effectively, is currently seen as the biggest challenge for publishers. In statements from publishers it becomes evident that, in addition to the features mentioned before, users of EP products highly value frequent updating of online information. *Rhein Zeitung Online*, the digitised version of a local daily in Germany, changes general news two to three times per day and tries to put special events online within one hour.

The development of new and associated services also has to be part of the marketing plan and strategies of publishers. Even small circulation magazines have perspectives to develop new revenue streams and create and maintain customer services by providing them with online access. In the US this model has been tried by a number of small and medium-size newspapers that appear to be particularly well positioned to sell consumer Internet access in their clearly defined areas of distribution.

In Europe some online papers are also moving to provide Internet access. For them this is usually a business with no long-term perspective. Local papers are then competing with local Internet access providers, but are often willing to co-operate. Examples are the *Rhein Zeitung* and the *Vorarlberger Nachrichten*, both regional newspapers in smaller markets. If you are a subscriber of the print product, the registration for the online paper and Internet access are bundled in larger newspapers which face hard competition and price-cutting from new and established access firms, particularly the big telecom operators such as *DT* (*Deutsche Telekom*) or *AT&T* in the US.

Becoming an access provider cannot be a solution for every online publisher. Access operations are a special service and therefore quite vulnerable to competition in terms of price and level of service. In larger communities the Internet access market tends to be glutted. The Internet access model is best suited for smaller communities, particularly relatively remote ones that have no direct Internet access or as local access point to commercial online services such as *America Online*.

4.4 Elements of EP Marketing Strategies: Individualised Products, Personal Services

"Newspapers have been in the centre of their communities and we are trying to do the same online", states David Margulius, president of *Boston.com*, "Boston's community mega website". EP marketing builds on the hottest buzzwords for general marketing in the 90s – "interactive" and "integrated":

- "Interactive" opens the conversation between business and customers for marketing. It's the chance to get closer to clients, to present publishing products and services to customers and to listen and act on their responses.

- "Integrated" means that publishers can see EP and its marketing in a more complete manner, consistently strengthened by as well as reinforcing every other department and product and service within the company. "Integrated" allows a company to reach out to customers through advertisements, direct mailing, or promotion, it is sending the same message and encouraging customers to learn more about the product.

The interaction between company and customers enlivens the relationship between publishers and readers and generates a new horizon for those involved.

4.4.1 EP Marketing Model

Marketing models have to take into account the underlying product features. EP and TP products are different in a number of important aspects. It is therefore not surprising that traditional marketing models do not work well for EP products.

Current experience suggests that traditional marketing models fail particularly in the online publishing world as the example of *Encyclopædia Britannica* demonstrates: *Encyclopædia Britannica* did not use its excellent brand name in the TP market to transfer its position into the digital one. So it already had to accept the market structures shaped by its competitors, namely *Microsoft*. Having missed the market for CD-ROM encyclopaedias the *Encyclopædia Britannica* intends not to be left behind on the Internet. It has put the entire contents online for an annual personal subscription of at first $150 (a corporate subscription is $300), reducing it to below $70 not too long after. A 72-hour-trial period is offered for free.

The market model of the *Encyclopædia Britannica* makes it difficult to see some high penetration in the next future. There are, e.g., no price variations for those subscribing EB-Online for many years. If you paid for the traditional version of the *Encyclopædia Britannica*, which is around $2,500, and you also want to use it online, you pay twice for the same content. As a buyer of the TP product you do not get any deduction for subscribing the online-version.

The nature of the EP products is quite different, therefore requiring different customer approaches, different communication and pricing policies, and the necessity to offer new distribution and sales possibilities.

Digitisation and distribution by electronic networks do not bring established companies or traditional industries publishing books, magazine or newspapers to a sudden end. Rather, they at first enliven the existing markets, add new features and supplement existing ones, lead to a further extension of products and services and finally offer opportunities for diversification and the development of new markets.

Such a reading of the market development also suggests a marketing model which identifies four different EP groups based on the relationship to traditional publishing products. It accounts for the transformation of the existing industries and their pursuits of the new opportunities offered by computerisation and networking. New market entrants might find this model mainly relevant for the marketing issues arising from product and pricing policies.

Stage 1: EP as "Attention Grabber"

The key strategic asset of publishers in the periodical as well as daily news market is the tie of trust, habituation, familiarity and dependability between reader and print product. In this context, EP can be used as an additional "attention grabber" to keep or attract customers and deliver service entirely subordinate to the existing product.

EP in this stage strengthens existing markets and products. This is done via information sites on the Web or by offering audio services and touch-tone lines with basic information. Technical, entertainment and other special interest magazines are often using give-aways of CD-ROMs. These products and services are free of charge and assist publishers in maintaining customer loyalty, gaining an image of innovation and developing a record in working with new media.

Stage 2: EP as Supplement

Based on this experience publishers turn to use EP to gain additional markets for their existing products. At first, EP products were a close copy of the printed ones including basic elements of layout and design. The new products were meant to be recognised as supplements to the existing ones and are used to add some new market segments and services.

Examples are when publishers offer the headlines of their papers or magazines via e-mail or offer electronic copies of articles or of their special interest magazines. As in the case of legal reports these forms of use of EP keep the printed text as the master version of the publication of an electronic version. The main function is to reach customers in a better way, make the publication also available when not at home or in a more time-independent way, or to attract a few new customers. This use tends to mainly service existing clients in a novel and better way. Supplement EP products provide some added value to customers. Generally, the cost of EP supplements is included in that of the print product or they are offered entirely for free.

Stage 3: EP as Extension

Supplements become significant extensions of existing products when publishers start to view and treat them separate and seek to market them separately from their traditional goods. New products or services are based on existing ones and compliment them satisfying new customer needs.

A good number of publishers, particularly the quality newspapers and wire services, have already entered this stage five or eight years ago by merchandizing their electronic newspaper archives and making them available to outsiders as searchable databases. Such news archives build on the digital versions of the daily print product, but they offer new ways of using contents.

In further extensions archives are thematically grouped and made available on CD-ROM for encyclopaedic or educational purposes. A further step is to provide magazines, papers or selected chapters of books online and to add – to the provision of information – the possibilities of feedback and interaction with editors, reporters and in a further step with circulation or advertising departments.

The pricing of the extensions often consists of flat fees and/or a product or service measure fee on the basis of time or volume of use. Most online papers are extensions to the traditional core products such as the *Chicago Tribune Online Edition* or the *New York Times Online,* or in the case of magazines, *Der Spiegel* or *FOCUS,* using the brand name of the print product in the electronic realm. The EP products have different content (fewer articles with a higher depth covering a different area of interest) and integrate interactivity and multimedia in basic forms.

Developing and operating EP extensions requires considerable investments and can be sustained only in conjunction with the continued support from existing publishing operations and helpful cross subsidizing in operations, marketing and customer service. Online papers are new and have great difficulties to generate profits. Usually the online services are financed with risk capital from the publishers.

Stage 4: EP as Diversification

Having experience in EP and finding new market prospects, publishers might develop new publishing products which do not take their formal or content lead from the traditional products but have their own product or service identity and use multimedia to a much greater extent.

While these products might still be marketed by bundling, they depend on new production, design and distribution technologies and have a pricing policy of their own. The task is to create new products with advanced multimedia features for new markets. These products require substantially new skills and capabilities from online-authoring to virtual reality technologies.

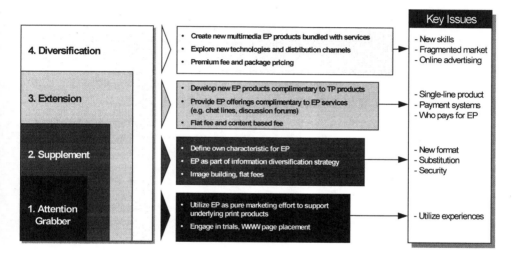

Figure 7: EP Marketing Model

4.4.2 Demand for Individualisation

The above-shown stages in market and product development reflect the supply side changes. On the demand side one can also see considerable changes resulting from the new media technologies. While the old media allowed the use of the electronic means of production and distribution only for mass markets and products, the new media allow for a personalization of products which turn them literally into individualized services.

Profound social changes correspond with the technologies' possibilities. Individualisation is more than just a passing trend. It is altering the way we live and what we consider as common. The chart below identifies the drivers for individualisation.

Social individualisation is made possible and reflected in the personalization of EP. The technical opportunities allow a high degree of customised services such as searchable archives, personalised clipping agents (e.g. *DowVision* of Dow & Jones) or personalised newspapers (*Personal Journal of Dow & Jones*).

Table 3: Drivers for Individualisation

• Social Changes	Multiple jobs, reduced leisure time, and fragmented interests are driving disconnection; increasingly, users will want communication and interactivity content to fill this gap. Higher educational standards and larger base of common knowledge will fuel demand for tailored and interpreted information.
• Telecommuting	The rapid growth of the cellular market illustrates the enormous demand for "any time, any place, any form" access to information and communication.
• Service-based Differentiation	As both access and basic information become commodities and change to becoming free, publishers will have to compete on their ability to respond individual needs.
• Interactivity	Ubiquitous, interactive technology will create demand for content that engages the reader and combines with communication.
• Micro-targeted Communities	With improved knowledge of individual users' interests, publishers will have to create "demassified" products on a very broad range of subjects and information communities around them.

Apart from the general social changes there are important technological and economic drivers making individualisation a key factor for publishing and EP marketing. Product design is, apart from pricing, one of the main keys to meet customer demand. EP products allow publishers a new flexibility to satisfy special needs through high adaptation capability.

The progressing individualisation results in the increasing social and geographic mobility which loosens the ties of readers to their newspapers. As a consequence professional and SOHO markets, for instance, require customisation of EP products due to individualised needs. A combination of local content and customisation, context and community can be considered to generate profits and shareholders value.

4.4.3 Developing Online Platforms

EP products are known to have difficulty to succeed if they have to attract customer attention and online traffic on their own. Publishers find themselves in the same situation as a restaurant owner asking the question "Is good food enough to make the restaurant?". While content is key and driving integration of industries, a sound product policy needs to add to the core content special measures to stimulate demand and traffic.

Convergence of industries will be achieved via common access provision and service platforms that integrate communication, entertainment, information and transaction needs. Integrating an EP product or an online service into such a service platform with other providers of information, communication, entertainment or transaction could ease entering and occupying specified target markets. But at the same time publishers have to make sure that their offer receives the attention needed from the existing and potential customers. Publishers' co-operations with public institutions such as hospitals or local service companies such as travel agencies or concert / theatre organisers have proven to be successful in this respect.

Online service platforms can address homogenous user groups allowing more customised products. This advantage is key to the success of commercial online services. The basic elements of such an online platform are:

- INFORMATION: news, program for music, movies or theatres;

- COMMUNICATION: moderated or non-moderated chat lines for users (it is often argued that journalists themselves could moderate a chat-line to increase the usership binding of the online paper); e-mail between editors and users of the online papers; increased capabilities such as video chats or unified messaging systems.

- ENTERTAINMENT: online games; interactive chess, interactive adventure games such as *MOOs and MUDs, Outlands,* etc. ;

- TRANSACTIONS: payment and billing services; electronic shops; software for public administration; paid government services.

Customisation allows the adoption of general services to individual needs while at the same time providing a broader context for intelligibility and usefulness. In the combination of information exchanges, entertainment consumption, transaction processing and communicative interaction users define their social world and network and construct the communities they wish to belong to. Successful publishers will always take this dimension of community creation into account in order to achieve the ties between reader and product/service essential to long-term viability.

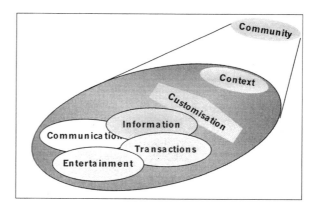

Figure 8: Model of Online Platforms

The possibilities of how to deliver the news online have incited many new services which customise the news to an individual's specific needs. As business life becomes more hectic, it has become very important for businesses and professionals to get their news and information quickly and efficiently. Customisation practically means adapting the EP products to highly individualised needs.

In April 1995 already, the US-based *Individual Inc.* released the EP product *NewsPage, www.newspage.com*, a World Wide Web news service that was chosen the "best Online News Service" by *Internet World Magazine*. Less than a year later *Individual* followed with a new product called *NewsPage Direct*, an e-mail enhancement of *NewsPage* for the single "knowledge workers". This EP service/product allowed the user to build personalised news profiles with up to 10 news topics selected from *Individual*'s library of 2,500 topics. The subscribers received the news via e-mail every weekday morning. Every day the company got more than 20,000 news stories. They filed them and delivered the most relevant ones to the user's mailbox. The news was broken up into 2,500 topics. Personalisation was done by limited selection of 10 favourite topics. *NewsPage Direct* is like a daily scanner of what is going on in the world that is also non-intrusive. The user can access it whenever she/he has got time and archive material for later reading. Customisation keeps the archive manageable and small.

Investor's Insight, discontinued August 1998, provided a similar service mainly for financial news and money services. It allowed a menu driven survey of individualized portfolios with automatic stock market updates and graphic representations of prices and indices. The service had access to over 16,000 databases and personalized scans to update investment decisions. It was advertised across North America over a cable network news channel and was less than ten dollars a month for basic service with a limited number of updates.

Dow & Jones offers the *Dow Jones Business Information Services* (BIS) as its own electronic product line. BIS provides business and financial news and information products to corporations and consumers through a variety of electronic media: computer, telephone, facsimile and radio. Dow & Jones splits the offering mainly in "Electronic Publication" like the *Personal Journal* or the *Money&Investing Update* and in "Customised News Services" like *DowVision* and *Custom Clips*.

DowVision is an information service that combines comprehensive business news, network delivery and a personalised filter to deliver customised information to the desktop. Using criteria selected before, *DowVision* alerts the user to news that directly affects the filtered areas of interest from a significant announcement by a competitor to an executive appointment at a client, from new tax regulations to the periodic swings of the stock market.

Personal Journal – "published for a circulation of one" – presents a combination of selected *Wall Street Journal* editorial, business and worldwide news summaries, stock and mutual fund quotes, sports and weather. *Personal Journal* offers both a first-in-the-morning news summary and late breaking news updates around the clock, 24 hours a day, 7 days a week. The basic price includes one edition every business day. Updates are available around the clock for an additional fee.

Another example: *FishWrap* was an experimental electronic newspaper system available at MIT. It attempted to address the needs of the freshman integrating into the MIT community by balancing an individual's desire for personalisation with the need to participate and know about the world at large. Starting in fall 1993, the MIT community used the prototype electronic newspaper developed at *MIT's Media Laboratory* and named after a journalist's proverb: "Yesterday's news wraps today's fish." *FishWrap* provided a continuous update of selected general news items and features, thus connecting readers both to the MIT community and the world.

Newspapers excel at local community content. A fact used by "home town" papers across the world. Audiences want to know what goes on around them and need to know it for their safety and survival, as well as for political participation and enjoyment. Some developments show that provincial newspapers can capitalise on their skills as local information providers and on their knowledge about their region, both for traditional copy and electronic services. Models for electronic services on a local and regional level are:

- providing a local community information centre;
- starting up a regional or local online service.

Both models lead to the concept of the local newspaper becoming a local information electronic network, which might include offering public information through kiosks.

A good example for a successful regional online service can be found in the western most state of Austria: The regional daily newspaper *Vorarlberger Nachrichten* started *Vorarlberg Online* in 1995. It provided local content within its own online platform. The publishing house dominates the regional publishing market, owning the paper's own competitor as well as several weeklies and advertising sheets. The online platform has been quite successful and the publisher has moved to syndicate the concept, software and marketing and sold it to other regional newspapers in Austria. In 1996 it moved into Austria's biggest market, Vienna, and started with little support from other media *Vienna Online*.

Interactivity provides new dimensions in service policy. Traditionally, service policy is considered part of communication policy referring to information activities of publishers regarding the qualities of their product. In EP interactivity has become central to the product itself. It is integral to the very functionality of computer communication-enabled publishing and is one of the key characteristics of the new product and service dimensions offered to readers.

Interactivity fundamentally changes the role of the publishers and the business process. Publishing ceases to be a one-way proposition, entirely controlled by the supplier of information or entertainment. EP opens the door for two-way relationships and successful publishers need to find ways to manage these relationships to the satisfaction of their customers. Interactivity also means that the service of the publisher does not end with the distribution of the TP or EP product. Rather, the entire business process turns from linear production and delivery into a circular relationship of mutually managed communication.

The new technical opportunities allow EP products to be more than text-bound copies of the TP product. EP attracts potential customers with multimedia features. Smart use of multiple media forms combine text, sound, data or moving pictures. The software language *Java* has created a strong demand for more multimedia features. The offline forms of EP have a distinct advantage to the online forms which struggle with low bandwidth, metered usage fees and, in general, inflated prices for the telecom and cable networks.

The tools of the new media such as PC-motion, sound and interactivity are being broadly rolled out into the market. Key components for electronic publishing, e.g. interactive advertising, will thus be more compelling. Online network connections are gaining in penetration across Europe, signifying changing expectations from citizens and customers.

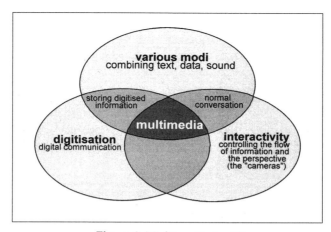

Figure 9: Multimedia for EP

The extent of multimedia depends on the targeted market. The function of the EP product for the traditional core products would also play some significant role. Many newspapers are loosing young readers. The online newspaper services represent a viable way to address young markets who can no longer be reached by traditional print products. Going online and providing multimedia and rich new media features does hold the promise to gain some of those customers which print has steadily been loosing over the last decades.

4.4.4 Communicating Product Qualities: Dialogue and Depth of Service

The return rate of users to online service platforms is crucial to their success. Publishers need to communicate the qualities of their service platform to present, former and potential users. Advertisers need to know traffic and usership behaviour in order to develop understanding of and build trust in the new medium.

Newspapers have a built-in advantage over other publishers when moving into EP: They can easily and inexpensively promote their electronic products and services through "in-house" ads in their print editions. With this marketing tool at their disposal, publishers can communicate to their customers – both users and advertisers – quite effectively. *Vorarlberg Online*, for example, is not only promoted heavily in the sister newspaper, but the publisher prints a monthly magazine going with the online service, being inserted into the paper and its local competitor, thus, ensuring a 100 percent penetration of all newspaper households in the region.

Self-advertising has increased in the last years. Newspapers spend half to two thirds of their total advertising effort on advertising in their own media. It is to be expected that publishers who are part of an online service platform will spend large amounts of their advertising budget for promoting these services.

One reason for this development are reduced costs and the potential for cross subsidy. Advertising in one's own media also means communicating with your own readers. This provides the opportunity to communicate qualities of the publishing company directly to current readers.

Print ads are powerful tools for sparking interest by newspaper readers who are not yet online. Ads combined with online links placed at the end of print articles which refer to additional material available online are a simple but effective technique for reminding readers – who have not yet discovered the online service – about its potential value.

One of the most common approaches seen in newspaper print promotion of their online services is in repeating the same ad day after day. The size of an ad is important, just as for any other advertiser. Steve Outing from *Planetary News* describes a Canadian experiment with promotional ads where traffic to a newspaper online service was tracked while a series of house ads ran in the print newspaper. Small ads (1/4 page) resulted in a bump in traffic seen on the site. When a 1/2-page ad appeared, the traffic increase was four times the burst resulting from the 1/4-page ad; for a full-page ad the result was significantly more than twice that caused by the 1/2-page ad. Even though he points out that this is merely anecdotal evidence, publishers could try this experiment in their own papers.

Announcing the publisher's online service or EP product to the world is done by using some traditional instruments, such as house ads in the own media, direct mail, promotions with computer stores and retailers, etc. But online promotion is equally important to getting the word out – and it's much less expensive.

There are more than 130 services on the Internet that will accept announcements. These include search services such as *Yahoo!* and *Infoseek*, the "What's New on the Internet"- and the "Cool Site of the Week"-websites, web directories, newsgroups and mailing lists. The publishers can notify these sites about their service. This gets the word out to the Internet community and – most importantly – places publishers' EP products and services in the databases of the many World Wide Web search engines. For most Internet users the search engines are the way how they find information on a given topic.

Getting the announcement can also be assisted by using systems that offer shortcuts in this notification process. For example, *www.submit-it.com* started as a free service and meanwhile turned into paid service that guarantees listing for your website on top search engines and web directories. This service saves SME publishers from having to research the addresses and submission procedures for various sites; you simply submit your site once and automatically register with hundreds of search engines and directories. Additionally, they receive automatic updates about their submission status, so they don't have to verify individual listings.

Involving customers and letting them use their voices might get them to return again. Online service can stimulate the interaction between users and editors and journalists, which is likely to create value and uniqueness of content boosting the attractiveness of publisher's online service.

New media offer to consumer and general interest magazine publisher opportunities for enhanced editorial dialogue with readers and thus enhanced mechanisms to understand reader preferences. This interactive dialogue exceeds anything previously achieved through "letters to the editor". Thus, editorial understanding of reader's interests may be enhanced and can be used for better targeting or sales of topic-related advertising.

The same new media that pave the way for interaction between marketers and consumers also give the disgruntled consumer the opportunity or the power to vent displeasure to an audience of millions. The President of *PC Flowers*, stressed that "if interactive consumers are unhappy with your service, they have the ability to log onto a bulletin board and inform millions of other members how unhappy they are with your service and what a terrible job you have done" (*Marketing Tools* March/April 1995).

EP allows for new services due to the various forms and levels of interactivity. Non-interactive publishing using multimedia will also have an online market among people who wish products and services to be delivered ready-made due to time constraints or for easy enjoyment purposes.

Interactivity alters the nature of the publishing product. It emphasises the service character and allows new dimensions of service depth:

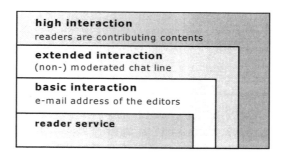

Figure 10: Depth of Services within an Interactive Environment

Service depth and utility will have to be considered as new product attributes and ultimately as key features for market success in certain areas of EP like finances, home gardening, and even cooking recipes. The following degrees of interactivity are being used by publishers:

- READER SERVICE: similar to that of TP products, it is used to co-organising concerts or theatre performances, and / or users can win tickets for, e.g., a football match;

- BASIC INTERACTION: at the end of articles the user can e-mail back to editors or journalists. This establishes the beginning of some direct relationship between online publishers and / or their content creators and their readers;

- EXTENDED INTERACTION: launching a (non-)moderated chat line, which is often considered as one of the new tasks of an online journalist. Journalists might not "only" write their articles, but would also offer their knowledge and experience to a (small) community of readers / viewers. It could be essential for increasing the readership /"viewership" bonding to the online service of the publisher;

- HIGH INTERACTION: users contribute to the available content of the platform. This also leads to a high level of customisation of an online platform.

4.4.5 A New Advertising Medium

Online advertising as a source of revenues has to be discussed in the context of an overall direct marketing strategy in the "advertising company". According to that argument, sponsors on the Net should look at their online presence not as "ads" but as "direct marketing". They are not just buying ad space, but creating a whole marketing program – defining the ways potential customers can interact as described above. This fact might have some effects on the attractiveness of newspapers as a place for advertising especially when they are integrated in a platform of "information–entertainment–communication–service" in order to create context and community. Realizing such a concept is impeded by some factors such as the insufficient possibilities to track website usage and, thus, to find an appropriate basis for calculating prices.

Even if links are sold, advertising in online publications faces a serious challenge because of lack of agreement and maybe also lack of understanding on how to set rates. A number of approaches seem feasible: Should the rates be based on the number of

- times a link to the advertisers' site is seen ("eyeballs");

- readers who actually follow the link to the advertiser's site ("click through");

- voluntary registrations ("client generation")?

The most demanding approach is to have a site registration required. This generates a profile of the users. For online papers it is increasingly important to get an idea of who the users are and in what they are interested. Publishers need this information to keep the traffic on their sites high and to attract well-paying advertising.

There is considerable debate over how to measure the contacts / visits to an online publication. The usual basis – except for certain flat fees for ad links or auctioning – for calculating advertising prices are hits, the number of times any information is called up and transferred from the publication's computer server to readers' computer client. This, however, may greatly overestimate actual readership. On the other hand, figures based on voluntary registration may greatly underestimate it. Other alternatives are:

- THE AVERAGE TIME SPENT VIEWING EACH PAGE. This gives answer to the question: What are people reading? Perhaps there are some pages that are requested frequently, but only viewed for a few seconds. This data cannot always be provided for technical reasons. It is calculated by recording the time between downloads.

- THE PAGE USERS SEE FIRST. Often it is not the homepage which the users see first. The publishers need to add some extra navigational aids and explanations to the first page viewed.

Sometimes it is useful to know how many of the users have their graphics capability turned off. This information is made available by comparing how many times the homepage is accessed and how many times a graphic item that appears only on the homepage is accessed. The difference will represent the required figure.

The advertising revenue generated for the online services have lagged behind predictions for years. This is not due to a lack of major efforts in that area. But online advertising has been given new life by Internet commerce. One reason is that Internet publishers currently have no other way to make significant revenues.

Only a couple of Internet publishers are significantly ad-financed, including *Vibe Online* and *HotWired*. These online magazines have particularly concentrated on "image advertisers".

It is debatable whether online ads will be an effective medium for selling products in the short run, especially given the Internet culture's aversion against any kind of "intrusive" advertising generally favoured by car dealers or fast-food restaurants.

Pricing the space for online advertising is getting more developed over time. Some time ago advertising space was often sold per thousands of hits without any further variations. New models arose like that of *FOCUS online*, a weekly news magazine in Germany (see below), or flat rates for advertising established by *HotWired*.

Playboy claims to be one of the most popular sites on the WWW, due to the fact that many Internet users are young males. The US site which was launched in December 1994 offers advertising in three forms:

- the option of purchasing a hyperlink to an advertiser's own website;
- a banner ad;
- a customised page of selected material from the *Playboy* archives. Hyperlinks cost around $30,000 for three months.

This site is attractive to big-name advertisers who buy contacts and address the target group of mostly young males. *Playboy* is one of the sites which are profitable due to its special market appeal.

Publications of general interest face a much larger challenge. For example, *FOCUS online*, the online sister of the very successfully launched German weekly magazine offered two forms of online advertising: the banner, i.e. a specified area on top of a page, and the button, i.e. an area on the right side of a site. Both forms are purchased as either static, i.e. without hyperlinks, or interactive, i.e. with links to the homepage of the advertisers. *FOCUS* places the advertisements in such a way that the areas can be seen immediately after opening the sites, therefore user attention to a certain extent can be guaranteed. Recently, banners have become more dynamic and buttons with animation and 3D graphics being used to attract the user.

Another method of pricing advertising space is auctioning. This is being tried by *Individual*, a US-based company already founded in 1989 to provide customised news services tailored to individual requirements, and also by *Netscape* for parts of its advertising space. Auctioning, however, works only for top sites and in hot market conditions.

The use of online advertising can be very different. In some cases it is mainly an information site on the Web and advertisers only want to show innovation or technical competence. It is an opportunity to establish an immediate and direct relationship between company and potential customers. In those cases, online advertising is designed with a high degree of interactivity and enables the advertiser to send information very targeted and receive market relevant information.

Generally, online advertising is comparably cheap to certain traditional methods, but this could change. Handling direct contacts, e.g. 350 e-mails per day, can be getting quite expensive since the advertiser needs to hire enough qualified (!) persons sitting in front of the screen and replying to e-mails.

Online advertising also poses a problem with the traditional business model of publishing. An advertiser might need only minor, inexpensive links linking readers to the ad's site from an online publication. This eliminates the publication's profitable role in physically manufacturing and displaying the ads. As Bruce Moore, Vice President of the New York agency *Jodes Advertising*, states: "We are currently building ads, and then we send the content out to the newspapers to publish the ads – along with 75 percent to 80 percent of the revenue to pay them to publish it. In the future, on the Internet, we will be the publisher, and we will get to keep all of the revenue." Thus, if the newspaper industry succeeds going online, it might escape the disadvantages of the manufacturing production model and the high costs of, e.g., paper, but it also loses the rewards that such a model has to offer.

Even if the websites of publishers do not bring much revenue, they can result in additional advertising for the newspaper. It can be an important additional service, especially for niche papers in high technology. The website also signals innovativeness and technical competence to the advertisers of the industry.

The key attraction, however, is to offer companies to publish their web addresses in their print ads. Those companies that do so – and agree to run their ads for several months – also get listed on the newspapers' homepage. US-located *Boulder County Business Report* (BCBR) was among the first to do this and provided it as a free added benefit for advertising in the business newspaper. The editor and co-owner Jerry Lewis believed that this policy would result in longer ad runs because advertisers want the online placement, too.

Advertisers, for their part, would prefer to put banners – whatever links are needed – close to content related to the topics of their ads. Readers of online publications view advertisements only if they want to see them. The advertisers can achieve a demographic segmentation that general circulation newspapers find difficult to provide.

Online advertisers are still experimenting with this new form of media communication. Advertisers need the help of experienced online publishers and agencies. President of *HotWired* Andrew Anker points out: "We have to help advertisers in the same way that television companies did in the 1950s".

Online advertising is for most of the current online newspapers the main source of revenue, "pay-for-content" will still need some time to develop outside the special interest fields such as investment reports or technical websites. The revenues compared to revenues from advertising in other media such as TV or print are tiny and they will need to grow heavily in the future. The key for designing compelling online advertising is linked to:

- integrating interactivity;
- combining sound and moving images and 3D animation with text; and
- authoring a narrative story.

Present advertising trends in the traditional media – newspapers, magazines and commercial TV – do not suggest a short term (five years) significant shift in advertising revenue streams towards the new media. In the short term, an overall expansion of the advertising pie is required, should EP develop.

The fact that there will be no major shifts in advertising revenue distribution between the media over the next five years should indicate the necessity for cross media strategies and strong innovations in format and content.

4.4.6 Distributing EP products

The Internet research department at *Yankee Group*, a consulting firm in Boston, already predicted back in 1996 that commercial online service providers need to move to the Internet if they want to expand. They stated that the online proprietary service model was bankrupt because:

- traditional online services charged users a flat fee to browse through content that is licensed exclusively to the service;
- Internet-based services allowed access to much greater amounts of information, they were more open, and search engines provided users with a device to sort through information;
- online services, thus, were pressed hard to justify their fees and moved quickly to provide Internet access for their customers;
- online services needed to focus on value added beyond providing Internet access, i.e. some specialised contents and services;
- Internet-based publishers made most of their revenue by selling advertising, whereas online services gained their major revenues from subscriptions;
- most Internet users were not willing to pay for content, at least not outright;
- the valuation of content and appropriate pricing models for EP products and services were a new territory for all parties involved in the value chain, stability was to be expected only in the longer term;
- the uncertainty of pricing models and standards effected all EP products and services, offline as well as online.

The commercial online services business had developed to relative maturity in North America with vendors such as *CompuServe* and *America Online* having over four million subscribers after 10 years of experience. At the end of 1995 the US-market for online services counted 11.4 million subscribers. Typically, online service providers gave content creators a cut of 10 to 30 percent of the connect fee based on how much time was spent in their online areas by members. Besides paying for copyrights, AOL, for example, supported publishers to go online.

The *Chicago Tribune*, which had been operating a service called *Chicago Online* on *America Online* (AOL) for several years, made a conscious decision to appeal to upper income readers. In March 1996 the *Chicago Tribune* launched the full-fledged version of a new website: *www.chicagotribune.com*. What made the site different from many other newspaper-inspired web services was its commitment to the high end of the market – meaning, it was clearly geared towards more sophisticated Internet users who had the capability and knowledge to view multimedia content using new web browsers and plug-ins such as *Java*, *Shockwave* and *RealAudio*.

The Chicago publisher followed a dual platform strategy, Internet and AOL: An online beginner might use *Chicago Online*, while a more sophisticated Internet user with *Java*-enabled versions of the *Netscape* or *Explorer* browsers might favour the *Tribune* on the web with real-time audio clips, animated graphics and interactive applications being available.

Pricing policy for EP products and services can be said to have been one of the most controversial and crucial aspects for the entire computer communication development right from the start at the beginning of the 90s. The demise of heavily promoted services such as *e-World* and *Microsoft Network* was related to the refusal of customers to accept the pricing models proposed by companies possessing considerable market power.

Pricing has been and will be a particularly uncertain issue in the online business. While offline EP products can draw on the itemized pricing and billing of boxed goods and shrink-wrapped consumer products, online services and products must be priced in an environment where the free of charge internet has set standards and customer expectations.

Various (complimentary and conflicting) pricing models have been discussed, but the key question always stays the same: "How much are customers willing to pay and what for?" An answer to this question requires that users know what to expect from an online publication. They should know what service in customising an online newspaper provides and what the value to them might exactly be.

Charging Internet users for information has met with substantial resistance, particularly among early adopters who have formed the "Internet Culture". The Internet grew out of the free exchange of information among academic and government researchers. Until today users steeped in this tradition, view any commercial activities as infringing and maintain that, above all, information has to be free.

But the profiles of Internet users have changed quite dramatically and a few Internet newspapers and magazines, e.g. *San Jose Mercury News* and *Raleigh News & Observer*, imposed fees on advanced services such as retrieval of items from archives. Others such as the *Norfolk Virginian Pilot* hide subscription fees in overall Internet access charges. Still others, such as the *Minneapolis Star Tribune* and *USA Today*, lead users from the Internet to subscription services requiring custom software. Earlier on, the *Arizona Daily Star* in Tucson directly charged a monthly fee for the totality of its content delivered by a standard Internet connection. The *Rhein Zeitung Online*, a local online paper in Germany, asked for an additional DM 5 if the user had a print subscription and DM 25 if not. Due to lack of success, however, the paper dropped the charges and has been accessible for free ever since.

Over recent years, polls such as the GVU survey have shown a continuing reluctance of users to pay for content on the Internet. One of the most stable characteristics of the surveys has been that one out of five users stated outright that they would never pay for access to WWW sites. This segment has even increased as the markets matured. This is not only discouraging for those who wish to apply a subscription business model on the web, but it may also reflect the perceived value of the material and resources available on the Web by its users. In consequence, most users report that their willingness would depend on both the cost of access as well as the quality of the material provided.

Paying for online content is a question of establishing the price sensitivity of EP demand: Would consumers accept paying more to publishers than to their cable-TV provider? The question indicates that customers determine their paying limits. They compare what they can get from printed products to online content. Publishers should develop the different added values of EP products and provide a new basis for pricing to the customers. When the EP product is a supplement to TP it is part of marketing. If the online product is diversified from the core product and enriched with multimedia features, a new approach is necessary. While many seem to accept that some form of fee is inevitable, many questions remain.

When a publisher signs up to be carried as a premium to an online service, fees might be shared. The *Los Angeles Times*, for instance, split its $6.95 fee for its *TimesLink* service with *Prodigy*. A variation on the subscription model allows publishers to keep a higher percentage of online subscription fees, but charges them "rent" and forces them to be responsible for their own marketing. This was the concept behind two new commercial online services launching in 1996/97: the *Microsoft Network* and *AT&T Interchange Online*.

Both subscription models seem tempting, but the idea of paying a premium on top of an hourly rate discouraged cost-conscious users from trying the service. That's why online services such as *America Online* emphasise usage-based pricing, which allows its members to freely surf from one online publisher to another. Under this model, publishers got reimbursed for the minutes users spend with them. Generally, the reimbursement rate was 10 to 20 percent of the online service's usage fee – about a penny per minute, based on a service charge of $2 per hour for the first five hours each month, and $2.95 per hour thereafter.

The usage-based model encouraged users to experiment, but did not provide a large enough return for online publishers who wanted to do more than tread water. Many experts expected usage-based revenues to decrease in the future. With faster modems consumers now download information in a fraction of the time it took some years ago, when modems worked at no more than 2,400 bits per second (bps). In a usage-based environment, faster downloads mean significantly lower revenue and providers might move to volume charges, i.e. charging a certain amount per MB downloaded.

Online publishers with highly valued content, such as reference works, began charging users on a per-document-transaction basis rather than on a usage basis. Fees ranged from 25 Cents to $1.75 for a download of a specialty magazine article. Most of that fee would go to the publisher.

Publishers may also earn revenues from online transactions. CBS, for instance, is making thousands of dollars every month by selling *Late Show With David Letterman*-coffee mugs and sweatshirts. Transactions on the Internet remain dicey due to security problems and the users' unwillingness to give out their credit card numbers. Such security problems should eventually be resolved.

Another important form of online revenue for commercial services is derived from referral fees which are known as "bounties". Online services generally pay a bounty of $15 to 20 if an online publisher can take credit for signing up a user via an advertisement in their print publication or some other means. Some publishers also receive additional bounties – up to 40 US-Cents per user per month – if users stay on for 12 months or longer. Such bounties add up quickly for major publishers like *Time Warner* and in the mid-1990s *Time Inc.* earned $448,000 from referrals to *America Online* and just $117,957 from usage.

Charging a fee for access to content on the Web remains a risky strategy. Publishers believe in the value of the content that they are putting online and they should expect to be compensated for producing it.

Generally, two main scenarios seem possible: The first is that the majority of the content is considered as "good stuff" but is free of charge in order to stimulate traffic for advertising revenues. Within this model the content is mainly or purely advertising financed (e.g., *Playboy*) or constitutes advertising in itself (e.g., *Sony*). This approach leads to high dependency on advertisers. It is mainly applicable to those consumer markets where advertising does not require highly specialised targeting and a high feedback rate (like 1,000 e-mails per day incl. some user profiles, cf. *USA-Today*). On the one side, EP products enable a high degree of customising publishers' services, but on the other side advertising will keep the mass markets alive.

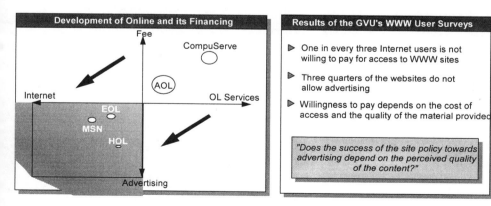

Figure 11: Site Policy Towards Advertising

In an alternative scenario advertising revenues are only a part of the total revenues. The main source are subscription revenues. This model requires a broadly accepted billing and security system. In detail: the general interest content will be free of charge and amounts to 30 to 40 percent of the total content. Premium contents, the "specials and really good stuff", are sold on the basis of, e.g., a fixed, flat-level pricing scheme. In any case, the middle term future of EP will depend on publishers developing paid contents – whatever the specific model might be. Over time, the publishers' function will be paid for: to provide reliable service, to sift, sort and have editor information, and to authorise and assure quality levels.

4.5 References and Sources

Bruck, Peter A. / Hannes Selhofer. 1997. *The Ignored User: Critical Factors Determining User Demand for New Information Services. Proceedings to the ENCIP European Communication Policy Research Conference 1997* (Venice, 23-25 March 1997).

Databank Consulting. 1996. "Review of Developments in Advanced Communication Markets". *FAIR Report Series* 1 (Oct. 1996).

European Commission DG XIII (ed.) 1995. *EL PUB 2001: Identification of influential technologies, impact assessment and recommendations for action.* [Report by Meta Generics Ltd.]

European Commission DG XIII/E (ed.). 1996. *Strategic Developments for the European Publishing Industry towards the Year 2000.* [Report by Andersen Consulting and IENM / Techno-Z FH F&E, Thomas Baubin and Peter A. Bruck, Austria]. Brussels.

European Commission DG XIII/E (ed.). 1996a. *The Markets for Electronic Information Services in the European Economic Area. Supply, Demand and Information.* IMO.

European Commission (ed.) 1997. *Building the European Information Society for Us All. Final Policy Report of the High Level Group of Experts.*

EITO (European Information Technology Observatory). 1997. *Annual Report.*

Kubicek, Herbert et al. (eds.). 1998. *Jahrbuch Telekommunikation und Gesellschaft 1997: Die Ware Information – Auf dem Weg zu einer Informationsökonomie.* Heidelberg.

OECD. 1996, 1997, 1998. *Science, Technology and Industry Outlook.*

5 Technical Excellence and Multimedia Quality. An Economic Perspective to 'Quality'
Alan John M. Donaldson, UK[1]

5.1 Introduction

The evolution of computer technology has taken place at a rate unparalleled since the Industrial Revolution. Together with telecommunications technology, multimedia is playing an increasingly important role in everyday life and suitable means have to be found in order to meet end user demands and expectation within the bounds of economic reality.

To anyone being asked the simple question: "Is technical quality essential for multimedia?" the immediate empirical answer would have to be a resounding "Yes!". On the other hand, a multimedia developer faced with the dilemma of how much effort to expend on development and programming might quite often be tempted to provide a perfectly acceptable workable solution that is not of the highest possible technical quality. The whole situation is further complicated by the thought that the end user of the multimedia system in question might, or might not, be influenced by the technical quality of what they are experiencing when using the product. A closer examination of end user perception of multimedia reveals that there are other factors that have to be taken into account in order to meet user expectations and satisfy their needs.

The perception of multimedia is highly subjective. No two individuals are ever likely to form exactly the same impression from a multimedia system or title, unless it is remarkably good, unusually innovative, or remarkably bad. Multimedia is still a relatively young dimension in the world of IT where it may be regarded as: fixed multimedia (e.g. CD-ROM, DVD, website), real-time multimedia (e.g. remote surgery, air/maritime simulators), or as public information kiosks. There are common themes to these types of multimedia, but they each have attributes peculiar only to them. Taken with the fact that technical innovation in the world of multimedia is "happening" at a remarkable pace of change, increases in end user expectation mean that marketable products necessarily have to provide intelligible content and be of acceptably good quality, and yet still be economically viable to produce.

[1] The author wishes to express his thanks to Middlesex University, London, and the European Commission for their financial support in the course of this research.

5.2 Evolution through Convergence

Multimedia has evolved from simple beginnings into highly comprehensive "media-oriented" products. Earlier arrivals on the scene such as games have extended their technical scope, encompassing later developments with greatly enhanced data processing, storage and bandwidth. Figure 1 shows a temporal representation of multimedia evolution.

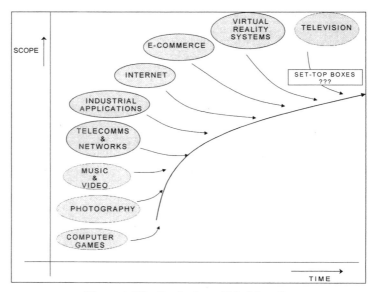

Figure 1: The Evolution of Multimedia

Today, television is the most popular medium to convey information, but its disadvantage is that TV-communication is still largely a "one way"-process only; the viewer is merely a "dumb" recipient of data without any interactive capability. While interactive-TV has had a troubled start and probably requires complete rethinking, multimedia on the other hand opens up a whole new paradigm for information dissemination where the user is an active player, integral to the whole process. Good multimedia therefore has to adequately cope with interactivity.

By its very name multimedia involves several digital entities (images, video clips, sound, text, etc.) which are integrated to give rise to an entity where "the whole is greater than the sum of its constituent parts". This can, however, be misleading: the world of IT is littered with projects that ran into trouble, quite a number of them having taken so much "on board" that they collapse under their own sheer weight (cf. Glass 1999). It is better to regard multimedia as a true hybrid that calls upon aspects of the technologies and traditional cultures of its constituent elements and, with time, is establishing its own culture.

It is important to appreciate how multimedia differs from what is traditionally understood about software and software engineering processes. Software has functionality and usefulness, but multimedia also has integral content that is often interactive. Multimedia content induces various degrees of expectation in its users, to the extent that it is helpful to regard the use of multimedia as being an "experience" that involves simultaneous use of more than one sense. The expectation invoked allows "trade-offs" to be made in the mind, where it is the perceived semantics that are important. An impressive "glitzy", high-tech multimedia technology cannot ensure that the end user is actually achieving anything in terms of knowledge, information, task fulfilment or simply fun/enjoyment from using it. There are a number of influences on multimedia creation and development which need principal consideration:

- technology;
- cultural convergence;
- market forces and fashion;
- personal and social needs.

5.3 Influences on Multimedia Perception

Some of these influences on multimedia development are complementary, while others may be counteractive. To translate this idea into positive actions for both aesthetic and commercial reasons, it is necessary to define a formal quality representation which recognises different ways of looking at a single multimedia product. There has to be an appreciation of the perceptive influences of the target market. These are: the technical perspective, human-centred perspective and contextual perspective. The different perspectives impact on the perception of multimedia quality:

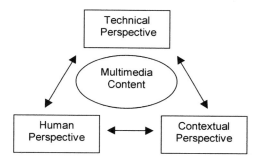

Figure 2: The Relationship between Multimedia Perspectives

- The technical perspective may look at the immediate physical, visual, and audio attributes and consider whether they are good, reasonable or insufficient;

- the human perspective permits an appreciation of issues relating to the suitability of a product for its target audience;

- the concept of the contextual perspective accounts for the fact that a single end user with a dedicated computer (top-of-the-range processor, monitor, abundant RAM, etc.) will perceive a product very differently from a group of individuals with communal access to a machine of inferior technical quality which is highly vulnerable to misuse and neglect.

Multimedia quality research in recent years has emphasised technical evaluation. Little work has concentrated on evaluating multimedia quality in terms of semantic impact. Research (cf. Donaldson/Cowderoy 1997; Zink 1993) emphasised asset quality and the technical perception of multimedia including interface features, search and retrieval functions and output functions. End user expectations and contextual issues have not often been addressed, although some researchers have produced checklists for assessing CD-ROM software (Schwartz 1993; Gillham/Kemp/Buckner 1995; Nordgren 1993). These cover multiple domains (e.g. hardware, usability, searches), but they do not go into depth. To achieve a greater depth in this area, interest is being focused on user-centred design issues which for multimedia easily translate into concept-centred design.

Users generally tend to associate quality with technical features in the first instance – after all, the most acid test of usability is whether or not a product will work! Previous research has tended to associate quality with technical superiority. This was a quite understandable initial starting point, but it may be argued that this view takes an oversimplified definition of quality by regarding that whatever *looks* technically superior *is* of good quality. Particularly in the field of education the true quality of multimedia content is often wrongly interpreted in terms of its apparent technical achievement.

A focus on the looks of a multimedia product avoids consideration of the *character* of the quality. While being technically and economically feasible to create good "quality", multimedia has to strive to be appropriate for:

- its context of use;

- the immediate environment of the platform in use;

- having the ability to satisfy the individual whims of the users.

A Raphael painting requires true colour representation, while computer games tend to require "jazzy" appearances and educational packages have to impart knowledge in symbolically meaningful ways. The necessary quality characteristics of these three products are technically, psychologically and commercially quite different from each other.

In practice, the technical, human and contextual perspectives have significant overlaps (Figure 3), but it has to be remembered that, e.g., screen resolution may be regarded differently according to the perspective from which it is assessed. The term "overlap" therefore only partially represents the situation and a more comprehensive treatment uses a multi-dimensional approach.

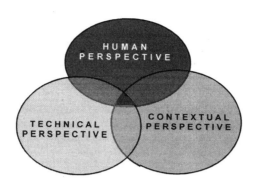

Figure 3: The Apparent Overlap between Quality Perspectives

In conducting research into these issues it is useful to be able to look at technology from different angles in relation to the involvement of the end user. It then becomes important to translate that into realistic and achievable aesthetic and economic goals.

5.4   Existing ISO Quality Standards for Software and Multimedia

To start to look at how the different perspectives may be correctly interpreted it is necessary to start with the known world of software and multimedia standards. A number of standards relating to quality have been used extensively throughout the software industry. Several of them have been referenced in work on creating a multimedia quality assurance framework:

- ISO 9126 (1996) proposes six quality characteristics for software products: functionality, reliability, usability, efficiency, maintainability, portability. These are then further divided into sub-characteristics.

- ISO 9241 (1996) uses the term "Quality in use" to describe the extent to which the system meets user needs for effectiveness, productivity and satisfaction.

- ISO 14598 (1996) is a set of standards that address the evaluation methodology. There are separate sections for developers, acquirers and evaluators.

A number of problems are posed, however, when ISO software philosophies are applied to multimedia:

- There are as yet no quality measures for some important sub-characteristics;
- the more "esoteric" aspects of multimedia are not covered;
- multimedia practitioners (understandably) tend not to feel comfortable with the somewhat "robotic" nomenclature used in software engineering ISO standards. While technically sound, their rigorous hierarchical structure and neutral language appears stilted and gives an apparently unimaginative way of describing the world of a creative discipline;
- usability varies enormously according to the type of user. This makes independent evaluation very difficult;
- in some cases the term "Quality in use" (ISO 9241) is very appropriate, however, there are other instances where it is difficult to apply. Specifically "good" multimedia gives pleasure and reward as well as being merely "useful";
- the software community distinguishes between *externally* and *internally* measurable characteristics of quality (typically source code) to indicate the presence/extent of system quality. With multimedia this distinction becomes confused. A more convenient distinction is between measurement of characteristics of the system versus characteristics of individual components within it.

To date no international standards are in place to cover multimedia's more "esoteric" areas. Standards developed so far only deal with specific technical aspects such as compression, CD-ROM storage and network protocols. This situation is partly being met by the creation of a new HCI-oriented[2] standard (ISO 14915) for Multimedia User Interface Design. Work on this standard is well advanced.

ISO 14915 (1998) details "Ergonomic Requirements for Human-Computer Multimedia Interfaces". It is split in four parts:

- Introduction and framework;
- general design issues for multimedia controls / navigation;
- media combination and specific multimedia requirements for individual media;
- domain specific multimedia aspects.

5.5 Balancing Technology with Involvement

The apparent shortcomings in the software standards do not reflect the importance of these standards in the domains for which they were developed. For multimedia, however, the ISO 14598 model of product quality seems to lack the subtlety needed for understanding and managing the many different types of

---

[2] HCI stands for "Human Computer Interface".

users, and the relationship between the users and the clients. It is necessary to model the characteristics of the users, as this can have a profound effect on the way that multimedia title or system is appreciated.

An effective alternative model to the ISO 14598-type of approach is to adapt a psychological model of how humans and systems interact. This recognises that there is a distinction between the system (and how it handles data) and the human interaction with the system. The Chapanis-model (cf. Chapanis 1976) considers the system and person in isolation from the environment. However, for business systems and also for systems used for specific purposes such as education the environment is very important; i.e. in some cases the role of the person is very much that of a machine, but in many other cases the purpose of the system is also to influence the environment by changes in the end user's behaviour. Figure 4 shows how this concept may be modelled for multimedia.

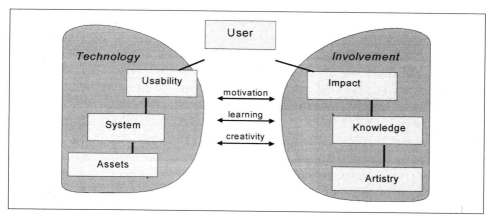

Figure 4: Balancing Technology with Involvement

This client–machine–user model of interactions is useful for discussing quality. In conventional contracts, the client purchases the system and requires suitable quality from it. Increasingly, the client is also seeking behavioural changes, and so they have to specify the quality of the interaction. This endorses the view that it is essential to be able to understand and describe end users and their behaviour within the ordered structure of a working framework.

5.6 A Framework for Addressing Multimedia Quality Issues

It is sometimes assumed that the multimedia developer should adhere to engineering quality practice, while the multimedia author is permitted to remain independent of any formalised concern for quality relying more on personal instinct and creative flare. Many of the quality-oriented practices described by software engineers have not touched the existing mature industries to which multimedia technologies are now being applied.

A frame of reference is necessary to make it possible to address multimedia development in a structured way. This has to be capable of assuring unhindered creativity while still affording economically viable and repeatable best-practices. The MultiSpace Project[3] (cf. Esprit Project 1997) chose the computer software industry as its reference because it is an area that is well-understood and has invested very heavily in deriving methods for quality improvement. The industry recognises a strong distinction between software applications and the technologies on which they are dependent. This also applies to multimedia titles and systems. In a heterogeneous discipline such as multimedia choosing a single frame of reference keeps any analysis manageable, although it still means that other dimensions have to be constantly kept in mind.

The ability to discuss and evaluate quality is essential. However, poorly directed measurement and evaluation can be enormously wasteful and expensive. Such a process must adhere to a pattern that points the way to how quality is managed. For this reason a quality view-point has to be built into the way people work on a project. This applies to all participants in a project: developers, content providers, publishing entities and the people used as representatives of the end users. The sequence for instigating quality measures remains the same, regardless of the development process. Figure 5 illustrates an approach now recommended from this research and builds on a theme first developed in the Esprit Project.

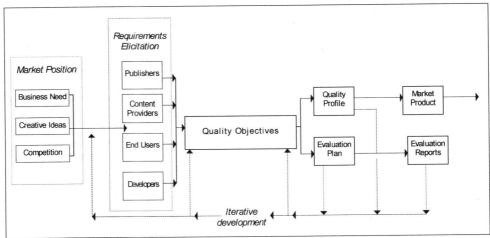

Figure 5: A Framework for Multimedia Quality Assurance

---

[3] The MultiSpace Project (Esprit 23066) was a European initiative to promote improved quality for multimedia systems and titles within Europe. It developed an approach for describing the quality of multimedia applications and systems, including the components and objects within them.

The framework allows quality attributes to be considered at each stage in the product development cycle, and each emergent product quality characteristic may be measured against a series of product-oriented benchmarks. In conventional engineering disciplines one considers having to deal with three active players in a project: the contractors, the clients and the end users. As can be seen from the framework, multimedia also has to deal with content providers. The methodology combines new concepts and elements with already "proven" existing elements (DeMarco 1982; Fenton/Pfleeger 1996) that are sound and practically applicable.

Within the framework shown in figure 5, it is essential that those using it should be able to relate to the original aims, objects and goals of a particular project, while still being able to take the project forward in the light of what is experienced in the course of the process. To adhere to the ideas proposed regarding users and their involvement with the proposed product, the technical, human and contextual perspectives have to be kept to the forefront.

5.7 A Tool to Appreciate Required Quality Attributes

Having identified a mechanism for quality management in multimedia, the focus then switches to how that is achieved at a detailed level. Towards the goal of a sound quality assurance practice different quality attributes of multimedia are being identified and hierarchically assigned to technical, human and contextual sets and subsets of them.

For example: The set of "technical quality" attributes takes in a broad array of items to examine. The subset for "visual quality" is further split into, e.g., "vision impact", concerned with the physical clarity and overall ambiance of the subject. An examination of "still images" is used to confirm physical qualities such as sharpness, but also checks if the product automatically allows adequate fields of vision and viewing time (or provides suitable control).

From "human" and "contextual" perspectives similar treatment is given to (e.g.) usability, hardware, local environment; following a broadly similar remit, which is devoted to how the end user responds within given circumstances.

Since good quality may reasonably imply a certain degree of acceptability, the first step has been to gather feedback from users and thus gain insights into which criteria may satisfactorily achieve the desired quality. This has been achieved through normal channels using questionnaires and interviews. From this a question format is being designed specifically to provide input for automated analysis which will then be incorporated into a software tool to aid requirements' elicitation, development and assessment. The intention is to provide a tool that may be used throughout the development cycle of a project and that permits those involved to keep the ultimate goal in sight.

The tool is being designed to be simple to use and understand (cf. Donaldson/ Yahya 1999), but the underlying research work involves a mathematical format comprising a series of hierarchical sets, subsets, sub-subsets, etc., which correspond to varying levels of detail for the technical, human and contextual aspects. A suite of equations is being developed to cater for each of the sets/subsets of quality entities and for the overlaps and mutually exclusive situations that exist. As each aspect is stabilised, it is translated into appropriate measures for use by establishing requirements, creating quality framework profiles and evaluating prototypes and products prior to launch in the market place. Adopting this approach allows the more "esoteric" aspects of the task to be isolated by a process of gradual refinement. The intention is to be (ultimately) able to describe all of the quality attributes in their widest sense in a manner that is scientific, repeatable and transferable.

It has to be stressed that this approach to quality management will not impede the very necessary creative functions associated with multimedia. On the contrary, the aim is to be able to assist it by having a thorough set of practical quality guidelines throughout the process. As an analogy, while it is possible to teach anyone who is physically capable to ride a bicycle it is equally possible to teach that same individual how to "play" a piano. But one *cannot* teach that individual how to make music! Only they can do the creative part themselves. But the better the support that they have, the better the music can be.

5.8   Recognising this View of Multimedia Quality Management in a Business Context

In order to translate the various technical quality requirements as they may be seen from their different perspectives, into practical economic solutions, the resulting quality profile has to be able to be actively used in a business sense. One effective method of interpretation is to consider the entire process from product inception through to market implementation as a series of hierarchical value chains. Value chains are used throughout industry and have been the subject of reviews for multimedia and ITC as in Porter (1998) and Coopers/Lybrand (1999). The highest (overall) level may be referred to as the "Business Value Chain" (cf. Figure 6). The quality of the final multimedia title or system and the economic control throughout its development and implementation are a result of recognition of the chain of activities involved.

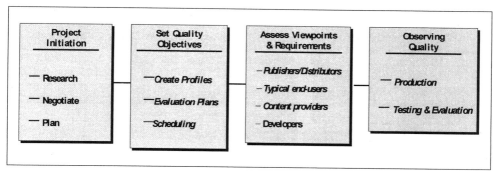

Figure 6: The Business Value Chain

The impact of the various elements in the chain may be all the more appreciated by recognition of their true value in the make-up of the product. Multimedia projects have risks associated with them and therefore it is important to be able to finely tune the final product to meeting the needs of: the market, the target end users and the agents involved in the project. The challenges associated with risk management are well known. Observance of quality criteria according to the framework described earlier, means that the subject of quality is *de facto* held as a high priority in answering those challenges.

The use of a hierarchical approach permits to cover the individual aspects of the overall chain shown above. For example, asset management plays a significant role in the overall business scheme and its associated value chain, often accounting for up to 75-80 percent of project effort. Asset management is a broad issue covering technical, administrative, managerial and fiscal issues. It includes, for example, configuration management, version management and fault logging. It also includes the ever-present IPR issues relating to the purchasing, hiring and licensing of "original" assets, used as input.

Figure 7 shows how an asset value chain may be represented:

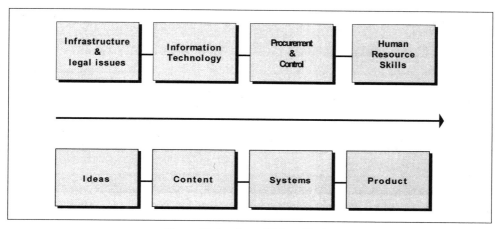

Figure 7: An Asset Value Chain

In the value chain such as shown above, an efficient asset management system can help to avoid enormous costs and waste due to reworking and purchasing items that are later abandoned.

5.9 Conclusion

The discussion about value chains has come a long way from the initial thoughts about multimedia technology and how it is perceived by end users. However, it is only if those involved in the project life-cycle are interested to fully appreciate the results of their decisions that multimedia quality assurance will become a reality in the final analysis. Indeed, the emergence of a "multimedia culture" has accompanied the development of products throughout which technology has become far more complex.

Technical excellence is essential to any good multimedia product, but this is by no means the end of the story. Technical quality may quite rightly be regarded as the "lowest common denominator" in multimedia, but other factors have profound economic impacts. These influence the entire product development life cycle and the end user perception and consequent market acceptance. It is therefore incumbent on all involved in the multimedia business and development life cycle to pay due respect to a broad range of quality issues in the quest to achieve an effective, economical product that is successful in the market place.

5.10 References

Chapanis. 1976. *Handbook of Industrial and Organizational Psychology*. Chicago.

Coopers/Lybrand. 1999. *The focus for Australian investment in Multimedia Content, Part IV - The Interactive Multimedia Industry Today*. [Multimedia Industry Group Report for the Australian Government]. Available at:
http://www.dist.gov.au/pubs/reports/excon/exconmm4.html

DeMarco, T. 1982. *Controlling Software Projects: Management, Measurement and Estimation*. Englewood Cliffs, NJ.

Donaldson, A.J.M./A.J.C. Cowderoy. 1997. "Towards multimedia systems quality". In: E. van Veenendaal/J. McMullan (eds.). *Achieving Software Product Quality*. Uitgeverij Tutein Nolthenius Holland.

Donaldson, J./Y. Yahya. 1999. "Development and ongoing assessment in multimedia product life-cycles". In: R. Kusters/A.J.C. Cowderoy/F.J. Heemstra/E. van Veenendaal (eds.). *Proceedings of the 10th European Software Control and Metrics Conference*. Shaker Publishing.

Esprit Project (EP23066). 1997. *The MultiSpace Quality Framework*. [Deliverable Document D2.1P; K. Daily/A.J.C. Cowderoy (eds.)].

Fenton, N.E./Pfleeger, S.L. 1996. *Software Metrics: A Rigorous And Practical Approach*. London.

Gillham, M./B. Kemp/K. Buckner. 1995. "Evaluating Interactive Multimedia Products for the Home". In: T. Graham (ed.). *The New Review Of Hypermedia and Multimedia: Applications and Research*. Vol. 1. 199-211.

Glass, R.L. 1999. *Computing Calamities: Lessons Learned from Products, Projects and Companies that failed*. New York.

ISO [International Organization of Standardization]/IED WD 9126-1. 1996. *Software quality Characteristics and Sub-characteristics*.

ISO 14598-1. 1996. *Information Technology – Software Product Evaluation*. Part 1: *General overview*.

ISO DIS 9241-11. 1996. *Ergonomic Requirements for Office Work with Visual Display Terminals (VDTs)*. Part 11: *Guidance on Usability*.

ISO/TC 14915. 1998. *Multimedia User Interface Design*. (draft)

Nordgren, L. 1993. "Evaluating Multimedia CD-ROM Discware: Of Bells, Whistles, and Value". *CD-ROM Professional* 6/1. 99-105.

Porter, M.E. 1998. *Competitive Advantage: Creating and Sustaining Superior Performance*. New York.

Schwartz, C. 1993. "Evaluating CD-ROM Products: Yet Another Checklist". *CD-ROM Professional* 6/1. 87-91.

Zink, S.D. 1993. "Towards More Critical Reviewing and Analysis of CD-ROM User Software Interfaces". *CD-ROM Professional* 4/1. 16-22.

Section B

Using Multimedia.
Cultural and Educational
Contexts

B. Using Multimedia. Cultural and Educational Contexts

1 Digital Dread and Hyperbole. The Cultural Context of Multimedia
Paul A. Taylor, UK

1.1 Introduction

> Our historically sudden transition into an electronic culture has thrust us into a place of unknowing. (Birkets 1994)

> Our conventional response to all media, namely that it is how they are used that counts, is the numb stance of the technological idiot. For the 'content' of a medium is like the juicy piece of meat carried by the burglar to distract the watch-dog of the mind. (McLuhan 1964, 18)

Technology is seldom neutral. Despite cliches to the contrary, e.g. "it's not the technology that matters but how you use it", it frequently has profound effects upon existing social practices. In the words of Stephen Hill (1988), technology burns into the fabric of a culture "like a cigarette on silk fabric". Western intellectuals seem to find it relatively easy to accept that the culture of so-called 'primitive societies' can be radically affected by the introduction of previously alien technologies, but markedly less able to recognise that a similar process of cultural extinction can occur in technologically saturated societies. This ubiquity of technology in modern society means that our attempts to analyse it can be likened to the situation of a fish trying to theorise about the nature of water.

In a pattern similar to that of many previous technologies, the advent of digital technologies produces both fierce advocates and opponents: "techno-evangelists" (cf. Kelly 1994; Negroponte 1995; Levinson 1999) and "neo-luddites"[1]. Theorists tend to become either extremely excited or pessimistic about the possibilities afforded by digital technologies. The terms of the debate over new technologies, however, tend to be such that the neo-luddites who warn of their possibly negative effects on existing social practices are generally dismissed as doom-mongers. The main purpose of this paper is to open up the terms of the debate to give serious consideration to the warnings of the neo-luddites and to put in perspective the

---

[1] I use the term "neo-luddites" to describe those writers who can be characterised as generally pessimistic about the cultural impacts of new IT. They have emerged as a broad school of writers who criticise a range of IT impacts. Early neo-luddites include Kevin Robins und Frank Webster with their seminal book *Information Technology: A Luddite Analysis*. A non-exhaustive selection of subsequent neo-luddites includes Slouka (1996); Birkets (1994); Postman (1986, 1990); Sale (1995).

claims of techno-evangelists. After briefly exploring the nature of digital hyperbole I explore the notion of *digital dread*. I concentrate upon two main manifestations of it: (1) theoretical and fictional expressions of digitality's negative cultural effects (zeitgeist writings); (2) more specific fears concerning the negative impact of broadband technologies upon traditional forms of literacy. The former illustrates with "exaggerated clarity" some of the potential social consequences of new media technologies, whilst the latter seeks to ground such concerns in contemporary experience.

1.2 Hip, Hype, Hope. The Rhetoric of the Sublime

1.2.1 Hip

> The social impact of cyberspace upon the individual is only beginning to be understood. (Wall 1998, 211)

Digital technologies and theories/theorists associated with them are undoubtedly 'hip'. In the Hollywood blockbuster film *The Matrix*, for example, Keanu Reeves stores his computer disks in a (significantly?) hollowed-out copy of the theoretically abstruse *Simulations and Simulacra* by the avant-garde French media philosopher Jean Baudrillard. Meanwhile, even amongst the 'squares' new media technologies are unquestionably 'it'. In the USA, for example, former Vice-President Al Gore has made much play of his enthusiasm for the *Information Superhighway* and the *National Information Infrastructure*, whilst in the UK Prime Minister Tony Blair echoes Microsoft's mission statement with his desire to see "a lap-top on every school desk", and plans are put forward for a *National Grid of Learning*.

1.2.2 Hype

> Bullshit is the grease for the skids upon which we slide into the future. (Barlow 1996)

> Schools of the future are likely to be framed (or limited) by 'walls of the mind' rather than by organisational or building structures. (British Computer Society 1998).

Hip topicality may easily become hyped superficiality. An editorial from the British newspaper *The Observer* succinctly expressed the commonly held concern about such hype in relation to the questionable substantive content of new technology-driven educational initiatives with the observation that despite the increasing tendency to introduce technical innovations, "[true education] doesn't come cheap. It can't be done on the Internet or at Shopping malls. [...] Lifelong learning is in danger of being defined as having to spend the rest of our lives learning what we were once taught by the age of 18." (*The Observer*, editorial, Feb 22nd 1998). I suggest that with the advent of digital media, glib euphemisms, shallow neologisms, and inappropriate analogies have taken the place of properly formulated concepts. To add to our problems, we consistently fail to learn from our past technological experiences.

1.2.3 Hope: Techno-Evangelism - The Triumph of Hype over Experience?

History seems to show us that there is a perennial human predisposition to confront each new technological development with the excessive optimism presently being exhibited by techno-evangelists. Dramatic, but ultimately unfulfilled claims have thus been made throughout the history of technology whether the artefact in question be the microscope, the portable radio or the TV set. This is despite the fact that the likely direction and eventual form of both the technical and cultural aspects of technological change are notoriously difficult to predict and frequently the pundits get it wrong.[2] Thus, in terms remarkably similar to those now used in the discussions of new multimedia developments, 'The Microscope in Education" report of 1868 recommended a programme of national education that gave "preference to plans which bring truths home to the eye, and with this view it is impossible not to regard the microscope as one of the foremost instruments for the communication of knowledge" (cf. Spufford/Uglow 1996). Similarly, in 1922 Thomas Edison stated that: "the motion picture is destined to revolutionise our educational system [...] and in a few years it will supplant largely, if not entirely, the use of textbooks." (Oppenheimer, *The Observer* Nov. 5th 1997). Despite technology's frequently unfulfilled promises:

> When each failed to deliver, it was blamed on teacher resistance, or school bureaucracy, then finally on the machines themselves. Schools were then sold on the next generation of technology, as is occurring today, and the lucrative cycle starts all over again. (Oppenheimer, *The Observer* Nov. 5th 1997).

1.3 Fear of Frankenstein. The Literary Heritage of Digital Dread

> Gibson's extrapolations show, with exaggerated clarity, the hidden bulk of an iceberg of social change. (Sterling in Gibson 1986, 11)

> They have no clothes, no possessions, no family. They're like dead code segments, cut off from the rest of the program and left alone in darkness [...]

---

[2] Thus regarding technical predictions an editorial of the US magazine *Popular Mechanics* in 1949 stated the following: "Where a calculator like ENIAC is equipped with 18,000 vacuum tubes and weighs 30 tons, computers in the future may only have 1,000 tubes and perhaps only weigh one and a half tons." Meanwhile at a cultural level, David Sarnoff CEO of RCA in the USA stated in 1939 that "It is probable that television drama of high calibre will materially raise the level of dramatic taste of the nation".

I saw the features of men [...] who were simply living out their programming. (Smith 1996, 44 and 297)

Despite the perennial existence of techno-optimism, literary culture has historically contained an expressive antidote which I label "fear of Frankenstein". Buried deep within the cultural psyche of Western society there seems to lie a fear of not being able to control technological outcomes. The potent mix of curiosity, creativity and hubris quickly lead to nemesis as portrayed in such Greek mythical figures as Pandora and Icarus.[3] Jewish tradition contains the admonitory figure of the golem and Mary Shelley's Gothic masterpiece *Frankenstein* is still hugely resonant in our age of cloning and genetically modified food. More recently, the highly influential fictional genre of cyberpunk has continued to vividly express the fear that humankind does not always control its own digital creations.

I propose that cyberpunk's imaginative excesses are a potentially useful resource with which to better understand the underlying zeitgeist of the digital age and can usefully be integrated with the warnings implicit in the work of media analysts such as Marshall McLuhan and Jean Baudrillard. To some extent, the disorientating effects of new media technologies have made fiction a more insightful guide to the here and now of digital life than non-fictional analyses. This situation is reflected in the fact that cyberpunk first popularised the now commonly adopted term cyberspace and it has been somewhat mischievously claimed that cyberpunk can be viewed as social theory (Burrows 1997) whereas "Baudrillard's futuristic postmodern social theory can be read in turn as science fiction" (Kellner 1995, 299).

Perhaps the main reason for cyberpunk's appeal is simply the "exaggerated clarity" with which it explores the emotional and social atmosphere of a world whose paradigms are based upon the primacy of simulation over direct experience. This clarity of the first wave of cyberpunk, however, has given way in more recent works to a tone that could more accurately be identified as one of 'exaggerated anxiety' and which provides an important expression of digital dread's two main influences: the extent and the pace of technological change.

1.4 The Extent of Technological Change. Ontological Confusion

If we were able to take as the finest allegory of simulation the Borges tale where the cartographers of the Empire draw up a map so detailed that it ends up exactly covering the territory (but where the decline of the Empire sees this map become frayed and finally ruined ...) the territory no longer precedes the map nor survives it. Henceforth, it is the map that precedes the territory – *PRECESSION OF SIMULACRA* – it is the map that engenders the territory and if we were to revive the fable today, it would be the territory

---

[3] The continuing relevance of the Greek myths is seen in such novels as Richard Powers' *Galatea 2.2* which explores the intimacy of the human relationship with computers.

whose shreds are slowly rotting across the map. It is the real, and not the map, whose vestiges subsist here and there, in the deserts which are no longer those of the Empire, but our own. *The desert of the real itself.* (Baudrillard 1983, 1 [emphasis in the original])

I fear that reality is doomed [...]. The story took hold of reality's hand. Imagine. (Noon 1995, 203 and 303)

In recounting the original debates held over the extent to which photography might be deemed an art form, the German cultural theorist Walter Benjamin argued that the discussants were mistaken in their basic premises.[4] For Benjamin, the most significant issue was not the artistic nature or otherwise of photography, but rather the fact that the new technological process had exploded the very definition of art itself. What arguably sets digital technologies apart from many other hyped technologies is that like photography in Benjamin's time, some of the hyperbole may actually be true in the sense that digitality may fundamentally redefine the terms of many of our cultural debates. J.G. Ballard, for example, argues that the ubiquity and pervasiveness of modern technology has reversed our usual ontological categories. The traditional boundary between reality and the imagination has become increasingly and perhaps irretrievably blurred:

> In the past we have always assumed that the external world around us has represented reality, however confusing or uncertain, and that the inner world of our minds, its dreams, hopes, ambitions, represented the realm of fantasy and the imagination. These roles, it seems to me, have been reversed [...] the one small node of reality left to us is inside our own heads. (Ballard 1995, 5)

Digital technologies accelerate this effect and a significant body of cultural commentators have argued that conventional notions of reality are increasingly under threat from both the qualitative and quantitative implications of the simulated environments produced by modern visual media and computer technologies. In the quotation at the beginning of this section, for example, Jean Baudrillard (1983) uses the fictional world of Jorge Luis Borges, to illustrate the way in which the postmodern world privileges the simulated copy over the original. Umberto Eco (1987) has pursued similar themes with his notion that we increasingly live in a world where simulated environments are not premised upon an a priori reality, rather we are surrounded by copies that have no original reference point: we live in the hyperreal.

This reversal of causality between reality and its representations simultaneously causes great excitement and concern. The excitement stems from the pace of this ontological reversal (cf. next section), the concern stems from the degree to which digitally sponsored change fundamentally undercuts our conventional frame of reference. William Gibson is the most famous of the cyberpunk authors whose work has captured this iconoclastic zeitgeist but I would

---

[4] Two of Benjamin's works are especially interesting in this regard: "A Small History of Photography" and his seminal piece "The work of art in the age of mechanical reproduction".

like to draw attention to some lesser known but equally interesting writers who
have taken Gibson's ideas to their imaginative conclusions. In his novels *Vurt* and
Pollen, e.g., Jeff Noon encapsulates the thrill of accessing a purely immaterial
number-based mental space:

> Into a world of numbers. Falling [...] Twisting over again, trying to face
> upwards. But still falling. Turning around in a full circle, but no matter the
> direction I faced, I was still falling down, down towards the snake pit. And
> all these numbers floating by, pure and naked information, wrapping me up
> in mathematics. (Noon 1993, 330)

He describes the effects of digitality through vivid and startlingly dystopian
portrayals of a world where reality has become subservient to its simulated alter-
ego. The profound and disorientating novelty of this reality-reversal and the
degree of vulnerability it evokes is expressed for maximum dramatic effect in
terms of childhood bewilderment:

> Reality following the dream, rather than vice versa. We won't know where
> we are any more. One moment your best friend will live two minutes away.
> The next moment, twenty miles away. A map of chaos. The dream will come
> through this new map. The dream will take us over. We will be like lost
> children. (Noon 1993, 201)[5]

The most common explanatory comparison made in cyberpunk to convey the
intensity of such informational experiences is that of the drug-induced psychedelic
'trip'. Accessing information is like: "[...] falling into bliss and numbers [...]
numbers and bliss [...] the numbers overriding the bliss so that the whole world
seemed like a mathematical formula [...] full of a slow ecstasy it was, a long,
drawn-out parade of tenderness." (Noon 1995, 224) Despite their dramatic nature,
the relevance of such portrayals to non-fictional world of computing should not be
underestimated, as indicated in the following real-world experience of a computer
programmer:

> The world as humans understand it and the world as it must be explained to
> computers come together in the programmer in a strange state of
> disjunction. The project begins in the programmer's mind with the beauty of
> a crystal. I remember the feel of a system at the early stages of
> programming, when the knowledge I am to represent in code seems lovely
> in its structuredness. For a time, the world is a calm, mathematical place.
> Human and machine seem attuned to a cut-diamond-like state of grace.
> Once in my life I tried methamphetamine: that speed high is the only state
> that approximates the feel of a project at its inception. Yes, I understand.
> Yes, it can be done. Yes, how straightforward. Oh, yes. I *see.*" (Ullman 1997,
> 21 [emphasis in the original])

---

[5] The reference to lost children is a theme Noon pursues explicitly in a subsequent novel *Automated Alice*. Here he re-explores, in a cyberspatial context, the original *Looking Glass* and *Wonderland* fictional figure of Alice and her vivid experience of the vertiginous relativity of identity arguably brought about in her author's mind by the qualitatively new aspects of photography of which he was an ardent amateur exponent.

Noon's work contains repeated references to conventional notions of reality being undermined by decreasing levels of solidity. Ballard's previously cited fear of ontological reversal becomes a major theme: "These days the doors between the two worlds were slippery, as though the walls were going fluid." (Noon 1995, 92)[6] The fictional concerns of both authors are reflected in non-fictional assertions associated with the information overload digital technologies are claimed to have brought:

> The tie between information and action has been severed [...] we are glutted with information, drowning in information, we have no control over it, don't know what to do with it [...]. We suffer from a kind of cultural AIDS. (Postman 1990, 6)

Such cultural illness is a major aspect of cyberpunk's dystopian portrayal of digital society. Yet, William Gibson has complained of the "lost ironies" in his work, pointing out that the majority of his readers, especially in the US, have taken his depiction of the information rich future at face-value, celebrating it as something to be aspired to rather than feared.

1.5 Pace of Change. Futuristic Flu and the Dance of Biz

> Such is the paradoxical outcome of every revolution: revolution opens the door to indeterminacy, anxiety and confusion. (Baudrillard 1994, 24)

> He felt a stab of elation, the octagons and adrenaline mixing with something else. You're enjoying this, he thought; you're crazy. Because in some weird and very approximate way it was like a run in the matrix ... it was possible to see Ninsei as a field of data ... Then you could throw yourself into a highspeed drift and skid, totally engaged but set apart from it all, and all around you the dance of biz, information interacting, data-made flesh in the mazes of the black market. (Gibson 1984, 26)

The much-heralded concept of the information revolution is inevitably predicated upon a sense of historical continuity with its industrial predecessor. The Industrial Revolution represented a qualitative shift in human affairs in so far as confusingly rapid social and technological change became the norm rather than the exception. Its defining quality became the way in which it liberated, in a hitherto unimaginable way, the transformative potential of technology:

> For the first time in human history, the shackles were taken off the productive power of human societies, which henceforth became capable of

---

[6] Further examples include:
"[...] the world is getting very fluid these days. Very fluid. Dangerously so." (Noon 1995, 101);
"[...] It was a fluid world and there was danger for everybody living there." (Noon 1995, 157);
"[...] the real world is up for grabs, especially since the world has become so fluid." (Noon 1995, 200); "[...] Even time was becoming fluid under the new map." (Noon 1995, 246);
"[...] Coyote is howling now, turning the road into liquid so he can glide down its throat." (Noon 1995, 254); "The world was dissolving and the new day bled away [...] safety, the rules, cartography, instruction ... all the bad things were peeling away." (Noon 1995, 278).

the constant, rapid and up to the present limitless multiplication of men, goods and services. (Hobsbawm 1975, 28)

Berman (1983) borrows from Marx the phrase "all that is solid melts into air" to capture the spirit of such fundamentally unsettling change:

> The intrinsically hyper-dynamic nature of contemporary technological developments provides one of the most concrete examples of Giddens's 'runaway world' where 'not only is the pace of social change much faster than in any prior system', so is its 'scope and [...] profoundness'. (Giddens cited in Burrows 1997, 235).

"Futuristic flu" or "retro-futuristic chronosemitis" are the somewhat tongue-in-cheek phrases used by Istvan Csiscery-Ronay (1992) to describe the even greater sense of dislocation that accompanies the advent of cybertechnologies. The "now" seems almost instantaneously and anachronistically redundant whilst the future is never quite within reach. Futuristic flu is cyberpunk's distinguishing leitmotif as it takes the accelerated socio-technical change of the industrial revolution to "warp-speed"-levels: "Night City was like a deranged experiment in social Darwinism, designed by a bored researcher who kept one thumb permanently on the fast-forward button." (Gibson 1984, 14). Elements of the future appear to have collapsed into the present and uncontainable, bewildering change becomes a self-contradictory status quo.[7]

The genre depicts a new experiential order where the boundaries between the real and virtual world's are blurred but does so with a sophisticated recognition of the ambivalent feelings of exhilaration and fear held toward that order. "Strange euphoria" (Gibson 1984, 19) is felt negotiating both the scale and speed of the "dance of biz"[8], the phrase used to describe the frenetic exchange of commercial information in the digital age. Thus the tempo of the dance is such that informational immersion is a sine qua non of survival and requires that you: "throw yourself into a high speed drift and skid." (Gibson 1984, 26) Frenetic activity is the background noise of everyday existence: "Stop hustling and you sank without a trace [...] Biz here was a constant subliminal hum." (Gibson 1984, 14) Life takes on the aspect of a feral fight to survive by means of constant movement: "To stand still in *The Gap* [Smith's version of Gibson's *Matrix* is like stopping swimming for a shark. You sink to the bottom, and can't stop moving again." (Smith 1996, 202). If we are to make the most of our new digital technologies it would seem that we need to learn how to control such speed of change.

---

[7] Themes which are further explored in the work of Paul Virilio (1987; 1991).

[8] The pace and scale of information in cyberpunk combine so that: "Program a map to display frequency of data exchange, every thousand megabytes a single pixel on a very large screen. Manhattan and Atlanta burn solid white. Then they start to pulse, the rate of traffic threatening to overload your simulation." (Gibson 1984, 57)

1.6 Jean Baudrillard. Viral Times

> No need for science fiction here: already, here and now - in the shape of our computers, circuits and networks - we have the particle accelerator which has smashed the referential orbit of things once and for all (Baudrillard 1994, 2)

The French media philosopher's, Jean Baudrillard's, later work provides an idiosyncratic expression of digital dread with respect to both my previously identified categories of the pace and extent of media-technology change. He compares the pace of technological change and its effects to the concept of escape velocity whereby once free of the earth's gravitational field objects enter free fall. Present day societies are presented as intent on acceleration of bodies and messages for its own sake and meaning becomes subordinate to the act of circulation:

> Things have found a way of avoiding a dialectics of meaning that was beginning to bore them: by proliferating indefinitely, increasing their potential, outbidding themselves in an ascension to the limit, an obscenity that henceforth becomes their immanent finality and senseless reason. (Baudrillard 1999, 7)

"Digital dread" is expressed by Baudrillard in terms of the extent of change this societal escape velocity creates. He describes society simultaneously suffering from extreme banality of meaning and an uncontrolled nuclear, viral fecundity of images and information. His analysis of banality describes how:

> [...] the drift of contemporary culture is from forms of expression and competition toward aleatory and vertiginous forms that are no longer games of scene, mirror, challenge, duel games, but rather ecstatic, solitary and narcissistic games, where pleasure is no longer a dramatic and esthetic matter of meaning, but an aleatory, psychotropic one of pure fascination. (Baudrillard 1999, 68)

This privileging of fascination over meaning is explored in a subsequent section in terms of multimedia's tendency to promote effects of stimulation rather than perception. Baudrillard's analysis of modern media's viral qualities prefigures the fictional explorations of similar themes in the work of Noon (1993; 1995)

> We are now governed not so much by growth as by growths. Ours is a society founded on proliferation ... today, power lies not in the real but in the virtual ...and an economy which is viral, and which thus connects with all the other viral processes .... Ours is a culture in which bodies and minds are irradiated by signals and images; little wonder, then, that for all its marvels this culture also produces the most murderous viruses. The nuclearization of our bodies ... continues endemically, incessantly, in the shape of our irradiation by media, signs, programs, networks. (Baudrillard 1993, 31-37)

The unconventionally speculative nature of Baudrillard's work provides good evidence of the decreasing distance between social commentary and cyberpunk fiction. Both he and McLuhan have been criticised in the past for their difficult writing styles, a charge which I suggest they would defend themselves against by pointing to our repeated inability to deal with the implications of electronic/digital technologies using conventional conceptual resources.

1.7 Culture Lag

> What we have today, instead of a social consciousness electrically ordered, however, is a private subconscious or individual 'point of view' rigorously imposed by older mechanical technology. This is a perfectly natural result of 'culture lag' or conflict, in a world suspended between two technologies. (McLuhan 1964, 108)

> The signal shift in the development of the digital culture is the loss of physical laws as the conclusive arbiter of action […] we are leaving the physical world behind, and with it the touchstone of physical and natural laws, together with the notion of irreducible limits […]. The law has to provide answers, but there is no consensus on what the rules are: the technology is growing too fast, and there is too much myth and ignorance. (Karnow 1994, 1 and 2)

We have seen how cyberpunk represents in a literary form the speed of technological change and the sense of dislocation it creates in the real world. In the context of the general confusion this pace of change creates, Marshall McLuhan compared the difficulties of attempting to control media developments to that of driving a speeding car whilst only be able to look in the rear-view mirror: one can only see, and by extension react to, what has already passed by you. McLuhan uses the term culture lag to describe the extent to which we seem fated to play socially adaptive catch-up with the technologies we create. A specific example of culture lag, is that experienced by law enforcement groups in Barlow's (1996) detailed account of the FBI's investigation of a case involving the alleged theft of Apple Macintosh proprietary source code by a hacker group calling themselves the "NuPrometheus League". His account also neatly encapsulates the generational aspect of culture lag. The FBI agent investigating the case, Agent Baxter, did not only inadvertently commit the amusing error of misnaming the group the "NuProsthesis League", but more fundamentally exhibited an older generations' ignorance of a digital world in which their young adversaries are completely at home:

> On the most rudimentary level there is simply terror of feeling like an immigrant in a place where your children are natives – where you're always going to be behind the 8-ball because they can develop the technology faster than you can learn it. It's what I call the learning curve of Sisyphus. And the only people who are going to be comfortable with that are people who don't mind confusions and ambiguity … We've got a culture that's based on the ability of people to control everything. Once you start to embrace confusion as a way of life, concomitant with that is the assumption that you really don't control anything. At best it's a matter of surfing the whitewater. (Barlow, cited in Rushkoff 1994, 11)

Noon's previously cited depiction of an ontological reversal, where adults feel like lost children, has a mirror image in Barlow's description of a generational reversal whereby such children are more acclimatised to information technology than their elders. My favourite example of this phenomenon was provided by Robert Morris Snr., a chief scientific advisor to the US National Security Agency. When questioned as whether he was concerned that young hackers seemed to be compromising the country's computer security, he stated that:

> The notion that we are raising a generation of children so technically sophisticated that they can outwit the best efforts of the security specialists of America's largest corporations and the military is utter nonsense. I wish it were true. That would bode well for the technological future of the country. (cited in Taylor 1999, 161)

Unfortunately for Robert Morris Snr., only five years later, his son Robert Morris Jnr. was responsible for the spread of the Internet worm which caused widespread disruption of US computer systems.

In the work of the most recent cyberpunk authors, the initial tone of cyber-exhilaration gives way to one that is more anxiety-ridden as simulation increasingly threatens reality. In the neo-cyberpunk novel *Spares*, for example, Gibson's concept of *The Matrix* is reimagined as *The Gap*, the place where you learnt that those three words "cohesion, order, chronology" meant nothing at all. (cf. Smith 1996, 208). Smith dramatises Barlow's notion of the immigrant's terror using a psychoanalytical approach suffused with images redolent of the Vietnam War. Those sent to *The Gap* to fight as cybersoldiers felt that:

> Somehow the reality of it [w]as always just around the corner, or hidden under a layer of light. We couldn't trust the people, we couldn't trust the land, and in the end we couldn't even trust ourselves. (Smith 1996, 204)

The description of the soldiers' fear echoes Noon's previously quoted use of childhood bewilderment: "We were like baffled, terrified children alone in a dark multi-storey car park full of sadists." (Smith 1996, 204) Despite such fictional and futuristic imagery, cyberpunk's basic premise of simultaneously profound and rapid change resonates with functional, non-fictional analyses of cyberculture such as the book *Cybertrends*: "Change - the surest sign of life - is now taking on a radically *discontinuous* quality ... Prevailing relativities change with the blink of an eye." (Brown 1998, 49 [emphasis in the original]). Thus the confusion the cyberpunk authors describe provides a highly exaggerated example of the changing media paradigms that have accompanied the advent of multimedia.

1.8   Digital Dread in the Real World. Complementarity and Substitutability

Technology burns like a cigarette on silk fabric. (Hill 1988)

There is a commonly espoused view which Langdon Winner calls the "Myth of Neutrality" and which I term the "Bananarama Theory of Technology". It refers to the belief "that in relation to technology it's not what you've got, it's the way that you use it and that's what gets results". In other words, technology itself is held to be neutral and it is what people seek to use it for that determines the impact it will have. In contrast, however, following the lead of Marshall McLuhan, writers such as Langdon Winner and Neil Postman argue that technology may be neither good, nor bad, nor neutral. In other words: how you seek to use technology may not be the dominant factor, it may in fact have inherent properties irrespective of how you seek to use it. A central tenet of this school of thought that holds technology to be non-neutral is the idea that technological systems carry embodied within them certain cultural values and assumptions that once released into another cultural context can have significant consequences.

The most dramatic illustrations of this process of cultural extinction are the socially destructive experiences of developing countries caused by the introduction of technologies from developed Western countries. These examples range from the introduction of snowmobiles to the Laplanders to the socially disruptive effects caused to traditional fishing communities with the advent of the motorboat. What is important for the purposes of this paper is that the cultural impact of technology is not limited to lesser developed communities. Whilst the effect on such cultures is easier to see because of the relative lack of previous technology, it would be surprising if the developed West's various cultures were somehow immune to the impact of technology. Thus, it can be argued that new multimedia communications technologies are not introduced to a social *tabula rasa* and it is foolish to ignore their likely impacts upon existing social structures and practices.

Despite this, however, present debates about the likely impact of multimedia invariably tend to be couched in terms of complementarity. That is, new technologies are put forward in the guise of complementing existing methods. In contrast, there is a strong argument to be made that new IT often acts as a substitute rather than a complement. This can be seen both theoretically and practically. From a theoretical perspective, for example, McLuhan argues that new media fundamentally redraw the previous working ratios between our senses. He critically quotes General Sarnoff who used the previously cited "Myth of Neutrality" to argue that: "The products of modern science are not in themselves good or bad; it is the way they are used that determines their value". (McLuhan 1964, 11) and asserts that Sarnoff's view "[...] is the voice of the current somnambulism [...] it has never occurred to General Sarnoff that any technology could do anything but *add* itself on to what we already are." (McLuhan 1964, 11 [emphasis in the original])

From a practical perspective and using the specific example of technology in education, with limited funding the issue of complementarity versus substitutability is thrown into stark relief: Every dollar spent on a computer and its software is less money spent on textbooks or other essentials. Todd Oppenheimer, the associative editor of *Newsweek Interactive* describes how in New Jersey, the State cut school aid and then spent $10 million on classroom computers, whilst in Massachusets a school district dropped proposed teaching positions in art, music and physical education and then spent $333,000 on computers (cf. *The Observer* Nov. 5th 1997). Similarly, in the UK the Library and Information Commission's Report of 1997 entitled *New Library: The People's Network* proposes a network infrastructure with £102 million net annual running costs, whilst the net UK expenditure on books is £31 million (W. J. West in *TLS* Oct. 31st 1997).

1.9 Dissenting, yet Misappropriated Voices. What's to Happen to the Old Literacy?

> The threat of Stalin or Hitler was external. The electric technology is within the gates, and we are numb, deaf, blind, and mute about its encounter with the Gutenberg technology ... It is, however, no time to suggest strategies when the threat has not even been acknowledged to exist ... I am in the position of Louis Pasteur telling doctors that their greatest enemy was quite invisible, and quite unrecognised by them. (McLuhan 1964, 18)

> ... The emerging information and communication technologies are the new literacy. (*New Library: The People's Network*. [The Library and Information Commission's Report 1997]).

In recent years there has been growth in the number of dissenting voices along with the large amount of pro-IT advocacy in the press and popular media. Ironically, this includes Marshall McLuhan who in 1993 was posthumously made the patron saint of *Wired magazine* despite being responsible for such dire warnings about the possible dangers of information technologies as the excerpt quoted above. W.J. West, a critic of the previously cited libraries' report, relocates McLuhan in the critics of new technology camp when he argues that : "The old McLuhan distinction between the medium and the message keeps coming to mind. The preoccupation with new technology, the medium for transmission of the content of books today, has replaced any understanding that there is such a thing as content at all." (*TLS* Oct. 31st 1997). Todd Oppenheimer, despite his close involvement with new IT, illustrates the pessimistic side of the debate in an article polemically entitled *All wired up ... Now I can be as thick as an American* where he claims: "The glorious high-tech schools experiment we are about to embrace has already failed." (*The Observer* Nov. 5th 1997).

One of the major causes of such pessimism stems from concern that traditional forms of literacy will be substituted for the unproven gains of what has been termed the new literacy in the rush to introduce new IT. Susan Bassnet, Pro-VC for academic quality at the University of Warwick, eloquently describes this fear with her observation that:

> It is becoming harder and harder for today's students, who I do not believe are any less gifted and hard-working than any previous generations, to read in a sustained manner [...]. This is our reality, and the clock cannot go backwards. But my concern is that if reading is always a quick fix, a five or ten-minute dash through a text cluttered with all kinds of distractions, will there be anyone left in 50 years' time who can read a novel by Thomas Hardy [...] let alone Tolstoy? (*The Times*, Feb. 27th 1998)

More succinctly, Sven Birkerts argues in the *Gutenberg Elegies* that, "The more complex and sophisticated our systems of lateral access, the more we sacrifice in the way of depth" (Birkerts 1994, 26). Educationalists seem keen to use new interactive technologies in the educational process without prior evidence of their pedagogic benefits: "If you have a hammer everything looks like a nail."

The adoption of Marshall McLuhan's work by the techno-evangelists provides a good example of the way in which hyperbole has tended to gloss over negative interpretations of electronic media. The presentation of McLuhan as an unproblematically optimistic advocate of electronic technologies has taken place despite the frequently ambivalent and admonitory aspects of his work. In *Understanding Media*, for example, he goes so far as to associate the likely cultural impacts of electronic technologies with two of history's most destructive dictators:

> The American stake in literacy as a technology or uniformity applied to every level of education, government, industry, and social life is totally threatened by the electric technology. The threat of Stalin or Hitler was external. The electric technology is within the gates, and we are numb, deaf, blind, and mute about its encounter with the Gutenberg technology, on and through which the American way of life was formed. It is, however, no time to suggest strategies when the threat has not even been acknowledged to exist. I am in the position of Louis Pasteur telling doctors that their greatest enemy was quite invisible, and quite unrecognised by them. (McLuhan 1968, 18)

The techno-evangelists, who have brought McLuhan out "from behind a potted palm again" (Moos 1997, xvi) repeatedly gloss over his more critical technological assessments:

> No place in the reverie of interactive computer-generated virtual reality do we find a warning that 'the pressure of the mass media leads to irrationality' nor the fact that it is 'urgent to modify their usage'. (Moos 1997, xvi)

I would argue that this refusal to pay heed to McLuhan's warnings is illustrative of the techno-evangelists' broader analytical failures and that, furthermore, his work provided prototypical evidence of what has only now become full-blown "digital dread".

1.10 Trivial Times. Stimulation at the Expense of Perception?

> With computers at the moment we're drinking a trickle from the fire-hose of human bandwidth. (Laurel 1993)

The metaphorical assertion above implies that the full creative and educational potential of computers is yet to gush forth. To unleash computing's full potential it would seem that we need to conceive novel paradigms with which to construct the new literacy so often referred to in relation to new IT, but so seldom specified. I predict, however, that some of the key cognitive implications and potential of multimedia will be missed due to the fact that its effects may too closely mirror the vacuous cultural environment which surrounds it. Postman (1986), for example, argues that the technology of the telegraph heralded the advent of context-less information. TV has further helped to foster a culture where information/entertainment dominates meaning and this influence is alive and well in the multimedia industry. The development of new intellectually credible design paradigms is threatened by the fundamentally limited conceptual boundaries of the present discourse. Inherent qualities of multimedia are likely to become aligned with wider cultural predilections. Thus, the lateral and stimulating aspects of new media, aligned with the visually sophisticated but conceptually shallow values of mass media society, are likely to substitute for rather than complement traditional linear forms of literacy.

The two key messages of the "multimedia medium" are its architectural emphasis upon lateral associations ("the hypertext paradigm") and the stimulation afforded by interactivity ("the Nintendo paradigm"). In an ideal world such "new literacy" would flourish alongside more traditional forms, but as this paper has pointed out, history is full of examples whereby cultural forms have been liquidated by the introduction of new technologies and the cultural values those new technologies tend to foster at the expense of others. More specifically, the work of cognitive scientists such as Jon Oberlander at the *University of Edinburgh's Human Cognitive Research Centre* implies that whilst the more spatially-able cognitive groups in society are likely to benefit from the new multimedia learning styles, the overall effect on the population as a whole may be negative if there is non-selective widespread adoption of the technology. In the search for a new literacy we should avoid eviscerating one that has served us well for centuries.

The predictive power of Marshall McLuhan's famous dictum ("the medium is the message") has been vindicated in an age that has given us the seemingly non-ironic neologisms of *edutainment* and *infotainment*: Form supersedes content. In a perverse form of synergy, the disorientating pace of technological change has come to be insiduously reflected in our social practices. Over ten years ago, the art psychologist Rudolf Arnheim pointed out the beginnings of this process:

> Educators know the problem of coping with children who inhabit a chaotic world … [but] there has been a worrisome tendency to believe that the best way of initiating their charges to the world they live in is by giving

preference to techniques and subjects that convey the violence of disorder, confusion, noise. It is a tempting solution. The teacher feels that he is keeping up with the times, and the student willingly relaxes with disorder rather than submitting himself to the challenges of organized structure. (Arnheim 1986, 237)

Arnheim proceeded to draw attention to what I believe is a crucial distinction that is often overlooked in debates about multimedia: the difference between stimulation and perceptual challenge:

> Stimulation is different in principle from what is accomplished by perceptual challenge, where an outside situation confronts people in such a way as to mobilize their capacities to grasp, to interpret, to unravel, to improve [...] there are education projects in which this seems to be overlooked. There are projects for centers of perceptual stimulation, pleasure domes of capriciously moving shapes and lights, dancing colours, symphonies of noises, textures to touch [...]. These expensive fantasies have, for me, the quaint aroma of nineteenth-century decadence, those refined fin-de-siècle orgies, which as far as I know were not held for educational purposes. They do point to an existing need, but one whose nature may be misunderstood. How many of our children lack sensory stimulation? One might suspect that most of them receive too much [...]. If we are not careful, we will entertain the senses with pretty displays and exercises confirming the children's suspicion that there is no connection between what there is to see and what there is to know. (Arnheim 1986, 238-239)

The search for a new literacy takes place in the face of the confusingly rapid convergence of various media technologies. Previous paradigms have been thrown into flux, in the words of an IT industry manager: "The power and sophistication of technology is doubling every two years. But the big uncertainty is the rate of convergence of current technologies such as fax, phone, TV, and computer". (British Computer Society 1998) Keeping with the fire-hose metaphor, there is the danger that without genuinely new paradigms, when the fire-hose is turned on we may become very wet but remain thirsty.

1.11 Conclusion

Cardinal Newman once said that Napoleon understood the grammar of gunpowder: If multimedia is to be more than a damp squib, more than just a slide-show with music it behoves us to find the grammar that will focus the nozzle of the fire-hose called human bandwidth. Despite some of the themes of this paper, I do not believe we are inevitably fated to repeat the mistakes of the past and to ignore the true potential of the present. We need to take a pro-active approach with respect to the cultural implications of new media technologies. This pro-active approach can be summarised as follows: a) We need to cut through the hype; b) we should learn from past experiences of technological developments; c) the pace of change should not distract us from its consequences; d) we should enjoy the new, but not kill the old. If we do not take this approach, the familiar deterministic language of steam-rollers will once again come to the fore. To show that one can be more optimistic than the neo-luddites without resorting to the excesses of the techno-evangelists, I conclude by quoting Marshall McLuhan once again, but this time with a much less negative tone:

> We are now compelled to develop new techniques of perception and judgement, new ways of reading the languages of our environment with its multiplicity of cultures and disciplines. And these needs are not just desperate remedies but roads to unimagined cultural enrichment. (McLuhan, quoted in Moos 1997, 137)

1.12 References

Arnheim, R. 1986. *New Essays on the Psychology of Art*. University of California Press.

Ballard, J.G. 1995. *Crash*. London: Vintage.

Barlow, J. P. 1996. "Crime and Puzzlement". In: P. Ludlow (ed.). *High Noon on the Electronic Frontier*. Cambridge, Mass.: MIT Press. 459-486.

Baudrillard, J. 1983. *Simulations*. New York: Semiotext(e).

Baudrillard, J. 1993. *Transparency of Evil*. London: Blackwell Verso.

Baudrillard, J. 1994. *The Illusion of the End*. Polity Press.

Baudrillard, J. 1999. *Fatal Strategies*. London: Pluto Press.

Benedikt, M. (ed.). 1991. *Cyberspace: First Steps*. Cambridge, Mass.: MIT Press.

Berman, M. 1983. *All That is Solid Melts Into Air*. London: Verso.

Birkerts, Sven. 1994. *The Gutenberg Elegies: The Fate of Reading in an Electronic Age*. London: Faber and Faber.

British Computer Society. 1998. *2000 and Beyond: A School Odyssey*.

Brown, D. 1998. *Cybertrends*. London: Penguin.

Burrows, R. 1997. "Cyberpunk as social theory". In: S. Westwood/J. Williams (eds.) *Imagining Cities*. London: Routledge. 235-248.

Coupland, D. 1995. *Microserfs*. London: Flamingo.

Csiscery-Ronay, I. 1992. "Futuristic Flu, or, The Revenge of the Future". In: G. Slusser/T. Shippey (eds.). *Fiction 2000: Cyberpunk and the Future of Narrative*. Athens: University of Georgia Press. 26-45.

Dery, M. 1996. *Escape Velocity*. London: Hodder and Stoughton.

Eco, U. 1987. *Travels in Hyperreality*. Picador.

Gates, B. 1995. *The Road Ahead*. New York: Penguin.

Genosko, G. 1999. *McLuhan and Baudrillard: The Masters of Implosion*. New York: Routledge.

Gibson, W. 1984. *Neuromancer*. London: Grafton.

Gibson, W. 1986. *Burning Chrome*. London: Grafton.

Gibson, W. 1987. *Count Zero*. London: Grafton.

Gibson, W. 1988. *Mona Lisa Overdrive*. London: Grafton.

Gibson, W. 1993. *Virtual Light*. London: Penguin.

Hayles, K.N. 1999. *How We Became Posthuman*. Chicago: University of Chicago Press.

Heim, M. 1993. *The Metaphysics of Virtual Reality*. Oxford: Oxford University Press.

Hill, Stephen. 1988. *The Tragedy of Technology*. London: Pluto Press.

Karnow, C.E.A. 1994. "Recombinant Culture: Crime in the Digital Network." *Defcon II July 1994*. Las Vegas.

Kellner, D. 1995. *Media Culture*. London: Routledge.

Kelly, K. 1994. *Out of Control*. London: Fourth Estate.

Kitchin, R. 1998. *Cyberspace: The World in the Wires*. Chichester: Wiley.

Levinson, P. 1999. *Digital McLuhan: A Guide to the Information Millennium*. New York: Routledge.

Laurel, B. 1993. *Computers as Theatre*. Reading, MA: Addison-Wesley.

McLuhan, M. 1964. *Understanding Media*. New York: New American Library.

Moos, M.A. 1997. *Marshall McLuhan Essays: Media Research, Technology, Art, Communication*. Overseas Publishers Association.

Negroponte, N. 1995. *Being Digital*. London: Hodder and Stoughton.

Noon, J. 1993. *Vurt*. Manchester: Ringpull.

Noon, J. 1995. *Pollen*. Manchester: Ringpull.

Noon, J. 1998. *Nymphomation*, London: Corgi.

Postman, N. 1986. *Amusing Ourselves to Death*. New York: Penguin.

Postman, N. 1990. "Informing ourselves to death". *German Informatics Society*. Stuttgart.

Powers, R. 1996. *Galatea 2.2*. London: Abacus.

Rucker, R./R.U. Sirius. 1993. *Mondo 2000: A User's Guide to the New Edge*. London: Thames and Hudson.

Rushkoff, D. 1994. *Cyberia*. London: HarperCollins.

Sale, K. 1995. *Rebels Against the Future: The Luddites and Their War on the Industrial Revolution*. New York: Addison-Wesley.

Slouka, M. 1996. *War of the Worlds*. London: Abacus.

Smith, M.M. 1996. *Spares*. London: HarperCollins.

Spuford/Uglow (eds.). 1996. *Cultural Babbage*. London: Faber and Faber.

Stephenson, N. 1992. *Snow Crash*. New York: Bantam Spectra.

Sterling, B. (ed.). 1986. *Mirrorshades: The Cyberpunk Anthology*. London: Paladin.

Taylor, P. 1998. "Hackers: Cyberpunks or Microserfs?". *Information, Communication & Society* 1/4. 401-419.

Taylor, P. 1999. *Hackers: Crime in the Digital Sublime*. London: Routledge.

Virilio, P. 1987. *Speed and Politics*. New York: Semiotext(e).

Virilio, P. 1991. *The Lost Dimension*. New York: Semiotext(e).

Wall, D. 1998. "Catching Cybercriminals: Policing the Internet." *International Review of Law Computers and Technology* 12/2. 201-218.

2 The Convergence of the Concepts of Theatricality and Multimedia Communication
Nicolae Mandea / Denisa Mindruta, Romania

2.1 Introduction

Multimedia communication is a concept that is increasingly present in the public discourse due to the penetration of informatics in the most diverse areas of symbolic creation, production and research.

The presence of multimedia-specific elements brings the problem of the visual and stylistic identity construction of the communicator in the space and the time of the communication act to the fore. Moreover, the way the communicator is perceived by the persons he/she interacts with becomes highly significant and the capacity to communicate is now a meta-criterion for the evaluation of the professional performance.

The experience accumulated by the tradition of theatrical communication (in a spectacular context, i.e. on stage, or in public space) could now be exploited by using its specific concepts in order to create new tools for education and formation with multimedia.

Thus, the main focus of our attempt is to connect the game/play paradigm with the cutting-edge multimedia techniques in the anthropological context of the contemporary communication and performing arts.

To think about human beings in interaction with a tool so complex and able to mediate the collective process of communication (creation even) is tantamount to apply Aristotle's terms focusing not on "what is" but "what could be".

The concepts needed for modelling this *virtual-veridical "what could be"* are: *the situation – the character – the action – the context – the role – the object*. At the same time the tool can't be regarded as such but as a medium able to accept and develop quasi-real events (in the logic of "as if").

The main working concepts conceived as a system of oppositions are *theatrical-real, spectacular-virtual*. The ordering criteria are the *degree of veracity* and the *compositional complexity*.

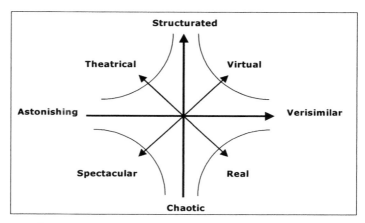

Figure 1: Conceptual Opponents to Map Multimedia Communication

In order to construct the model we start with the *theatrical–spectacular–real–virtual* paradigm and not with classical definitions for notions that are paradoxical from the beginning (such as Virtual Reality) or devalued through popularising uses (such as the dialogue "man–computer"). Having this axiomatic paradigm as a starting point, the model could be developed in an interdisciplinary direction.

Some of the possible dimensions could be defined through the polarities: *artistic–technologic; intuitive–conceptual; pedagogic formative–prospective*. These six notions form two triads: *humanistic (artistic–intuitive–formative)* and *realistic (technologic–conceptual–prospective)*. The cognitive bridge between these two triads is what metaphorically could be called the *narrative turn*. On the one hand, by introducing narrativity as a notion common to both the humanist and techno-logical levels we place ourselves in a discussion that requires us to use the notions: *hypertext, hyperfiction, hyperdrama* and their contextual family. On the other hand, we become engaged in the study of the emotional complex that is emerging in the interaction between man and the environment.

2.2 Computers as Theatre

The dynamics of the computer field has no other rival but the dynamics of artistic vanguards at the beginning of the 20th century. Its evolution is only partly technological, the true revolution taking place in the beneficiary field. As the programmer Paul Heckel states:

> The cinematography did not flourish until the engineers lost control in favour to the artists – more precisely to the masters of communication. The

same thing is happening now in the personal computer field. (Heckel, quoted in Norman 1984, 5)

Brenda Laurel's idea, original in its simplicity, is embodied in the title of her book *Computers as Theatre*. This book has already had six editions, an extremely rare thing in such a field. Its sources are at least two, completely different ones. On the one hand, as in all fields of theatrology, an essential source was the "Politics of Aristotle". Laurel takes the relationship between form and structure and the way in which the structural elements can be combined in order to create an organic whole (in these terms: the relation–collocation paradigm) and to be able afterwards to describe the way in which the relationship man–computer evolves. On the other hand, the complementary attitude is the one defined by Heckel in *The Elements of Friendly Software Design*: "When I project a product I think of my program as a show for the user" (cf. Norman 1984, 5).

Laurel's approach to the theatrical model follows a few steps which can be found in the methodology of several authors: the identification of a metaphor, its deconstruction, the axiomatic construction of the new model. The metaphor "All the world is a stage" leads us to a few concrete notions : stage, actors, characters, actions taking place in a concrete context, in the presence of an audience, notions that serve a certain vision on life. In the interactive process man–computer the theatrical metaphor is identified as an interface metaphor. Brenda Laurel also quotes from a study by Elias Horowitz, *An Integrated System for Creating Educational Software* (1988), in which the theatrical metaphor includes notions as "director" or "rehearsal" in order to create an educational concept as "programming by rehearsal".

The problem reaches a high level of complexity when it is regarded dynamically. Looking at a computer screen and comparing it with a stage does not say very much when this picture is a static one. Its dynamics correspond to a deep level of theatricality (narration) and this is the centre of the model (not the screen as a stage but programming as playwright). We are now confronted with two sets of problems depending on the static or dynamic character of the theatricality that these express. And we have to distinguish between the visual characteristics of theatrical ("what we see") and the depth characteristics from which the narration is the most important ("what happens"). The basic concepts of the model drawn out from the concept of theatricality are the "situation" and the "character".

The next step in our attempt to define the specifics of the theatrical model in multimedia communication is to determine the following elements of the "virtual character":

- the quality of attention and relevant reactions;
- the capacity to measure and integrate the characteristics of the human partner;
- the capacity to take decisions in a determinate or uncertain situation;

- the attitudes and what they reveal;
- the expression and prediction of intentionality;
- the role and expression adaptation;
- the unlimited variability in movements and reactions; and
- the coherence and stability of the actions and the goals.

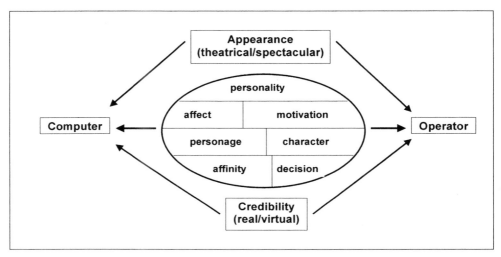

Figure 2: The Theatrical Model

The area of affectivity is shared between the "Operator" and the "Computer". This topic is developed in depth by Rosalind Picard (1997) in *Affective Computing* (MIT Press, 1997). In her vision a computer can be said to have emotion if it has five components that are present in healthy human emotional systems. The first of these is to have behaviour that appears to arise from emotions.[1] In fact, the most important thing is the expression of the affect, not the affect itself. Defining the affect as a result of an evaluation of the situation and/or a character and finding its expression doesn't mean that the emotional behaviour is similar for computers and human beings; it is the relationship that is marked by the affective responses in a shared emotional experience.

This approach to explore the convergence of the concepts of theatricality and multimedia communication has both a theoretical dimension in analysing the construction of a cultural identity in the digital era and a pragmatic one. For our university we see two pragmatic directions: creating new ways to improve the curriculum and introduce "Directing for Digital Media" as a master's degree in the Multimedia Department.

---

[1] For the other components cf. Picard (1997), 70.

2.3 New Perspectives in Education

The concept of the Theatrical Model implies a specific representation of the world. In this representation a hidden structure of learning is supposed: from the games of children to the complicated strategies of the mature human being, the concept of improvisation is the educational key for the improvement of communication skills.

It seems to us that for common understanding there is no connection between the computer and the concept of improvisation, understood as free imaginative reactions to the five senses.

The simultaneity of conceiving and performing (artistic or non-artistic) work, which is a process and a technique at the same time, implies employing human resources in a spontaneous and a surprising way in order to solve the problems created by the environment.

When the environment is a digital one the quality of the sensation is different. The sound, the touching and the visual sensations are linked in a virtual continuous space shared, in an interactive way, with a social being or a community.

In order to develop educational procedures based on improvisation we may think about multimedia as multimedia and to invent games and exercises in bi-media connections.

Classic exercises like those combining word and sounds, visual and sounds, body and word, body and non-verbal sound that we can find in such books as *Improvisation for the Theatre* by Viola Spolin or *Improvisation* by Hodgson/Richards must be adapted for written word-digital sound, animated body, visual representation of words and sounds, etc., all the variations that we can call "digital environment improvisation". The largest family of this kind of exercises known as "first thought, best thought" are improving the right reaction for a configuration of stimuli, but the games of identification (such as "the looking glass", "the shadow", "the director and the actor") are more expressive and more sophisticated ones.

In theatre we are talking about exercises without using a text and improvisation using a text. The theatrical image is conceived as a whole of verbal and non-verbal representations, but the idea that the word(s) is (are) visually represented doesn't make sense. In multimedia the word (the text) can be a sound or a visual representation (not necessary in letters).

It means that the situation of communication is different, the specific skills are also different but the steps could be imagined in a similar way:

- developing concentration and spontaneity;
- understanding the situation;
- building characterisation;

- creating mood and atmosphere;
- creating rhythm (visual and sound).

Let's imagine the following exercise as a metaphor: a "looking glass" adapted for digital environment. The exercise for actors goes like this: one in front of another, the actor that is playing the role of the "looking glass" must imitate each position or movement of the active actor. Suppose that a video camera is taking the image of the subject (from detail to the whole body), transferring it into a digital medium (it could be a 15-inch-monitor or 10-feet-projection), and the actor focuses on imitating his/her own image minimally transformed by specific software or by interventions of another actor. The improvising work of the actor is connected to the real world through his five senses. The cyberspace and the VR are the media sensorially interfaced with the actor. This situation is congruent with the definition of the multimedia domain: text, image and sound as a digital continuum, interactively structured.

Keeping all this in mind Art Universities with Stage Directing and Film Directing Departments should be fertile ground to develop "Directing for Digital Media". We consider this statement a starting point for new discussions.

2.4 References and Further Literature

Aarseth, E. 1997. *Cybertext: Perspectives on Ergodic Literature.* Johns Hopkins UP. [esp. pp. 24-41: "Textuality, Non-linearity and Interactivity"]

Hazel-Smith/R. Dean. 1997. *Improvisation, Hypermedia and the Arts.* Harwood Academic Publishers. [esp. pp. 52-53: "Environments for Improvisation"; pp. 249-245: "Computer and Improvisation"]

Landow, G.P. (ed.). 1994. *Hyper/Text/Theory.* Johns Hopkins UP.

Landow, G.P. (ed.). 1997. *Hypertext 2.0 : The Convergence of Contemporary Critical Theory and Technology* (Parallax Re-Visions of Culture and Society). Johns Hopkins UP.

Laurel, B. 1993. *Computers as Theatre.* New York: Addison-Wesley. [esp. pp. 191-192: "The Future of Mediated Improvisation"]

Milano, D. (ed.). 1997. *Interactivity in Action: Case Studies of Multimedia Masterworks Innovative Games & Other Successful Interactive Products.*

Murray, J.H. 1997. *Hamlet on the Holodeck: The Future of Narrative in Cyberspace.* New York: Free Press.

Norman, D.A. 1984. *The Elements of Friendly Software Design.* New York: Warner Book.

Picard, R. 1997. *Affective Computing.* Cambridge, Mass.: MIT Press.

Salso, R.O. *Cognition and the Visual Arts.* Cambridge, Mass.: MIT Press/Bradford Books.

Strasberry, D. 1998. *Labyrinth: The Art of Interactive Writing and Design: Content Development for New Media.*

3 Cognitive Processing of Multimedia Documents. A Lithuanian Study
Aukse Balcytiene / Dalia Svirmickiene, Lithuania[1]

3.1 Introduction

Most people think that they are fairly media literate. And this is understandable: We are able to use various kinds of media messages for diverse purposes, we are able to inform, educate and entertain ourselves. We know how to expose ourselves to media, we know how to appreciate messages, we know what kind of information is worth spending time with and what is not.

However, as more and more media converge, people will be required not only to learn to comprehend the meanings of messages transferred, more importantly, the awareness of effects of multimedia will be of critical significance. This is the time when media literacy enters the context.

With this particular goal in mind – to stimulate reader's awareness of messages transferred through diverse media – we attempted to design our research. The main hypothesis of the study was to present a multimedia document the design of which would challenge commonly held beliefs about multimedia effects, content and how the human mind works. Concerning the content presented in contemporary documents, it was expected that the specific design solution would challenge students to become aware of the learning process and, thus, would make them think of what they are gaining from the learning situation.

Although the major goal was to explore the cognitive processing of multimedia documents, it appeared that issues other than user characteristics need to be taken into consideration and must be included as design hypothesis. Early design stages have shown that the task appears to be practically unsolvable. Multimedia documents allow us to include numerous points of interest, therefore any group of designers is unable to control all critical effects related both to design and usage of contemporary multimedia content. This inherent complexity is a unique feature of multimedia which only recently was given a more serious thought by communications and media scholars (Fidler 1997; Landauer 1997).

As with any criticism there are inevitably positive and negative effects with multimedia design. An obvious, positive effect is that subjects taking part in an

[1] The authors are indebted to modern art critic Rasa Andriusyte-Zukiene for her support in designing the collection of Ciurlionis' paintings and developing the composition. The expertise of Egidijus Vaskevicius, multimedia designer at the Multimedia Laboratory of Vytautas Magnus University has greatly helped us to better understand the value of contemporary information technologies.

experiment gain something meaningful from the learning situation. Although one might criticize this presumption it is hard to imagine that, having access to new information, subjects could escape increase in their knowledge!

In this paper, however, the negative effects were considered as the more interesting ones: As a closer look at the learning process revealed that specific designs applied to multimedia documents are taken for granted and that designers have a few naïve conceptions about the readers. Although this design solution was seen as a main cause, it turned out that, when learners were left on their own, the reader motivation came from other matters. These aspects will be elaborated further at the end of this paper.

Three major steps will be taken in this paper. First, the general motive and the issues that stimulated the authors to design and use the multimedia document will be addressed. More specifically, the issues concerning media literacy, cognitive processing of interactive multimedia document and usability issues will be discussed. Several illustrations will be employed to make the debates comprehensible. Secondly, new interactive media and its suitability to manifest cultural heritage will be introduced. Thirdly, the experimental condition will briefly be discussed. From there we will pick up some of the arguments and will talk about the need for new electronic publishing models. Concerning ideas of how to promote reader's motivation, we will introduce a modified version of the multimedia document "Interactive Excursions to M. K. Ciurlionis' Art".

3.2 Cognitive Processing of Multimedia Content. New Opportunities to Develop Critical Media Literacy

3.2.1 Lessons from the Past. Are we Literate?

Generally speaking, we are fairly familiar with all kinds of media. If we take a closer look at how we spend our time with media, we can say that we know how to expose ourselves to media. We know how to absorb information, we know how to be entertained by the media. Although nobody has taught us exactly how to read a book or watch a TV program, we are fairly capable to deal with these tasks. Thus, we can say that we possess a quite remarkable set of skills: We are able to appreciate various styles in paintings, moving images, texts and sounds. Sometimes we actively seek media messages, we check new publications, we search for specific news, we seek our favourite programs on TV. At other times we behave passively with no conscious reflection of media messages.

TV and radio are two media constantly delivering messages to us. Contemporary studies on media effects conclude that television is the least intellectual of all media, but the most emotional (see Potter 1997; Gass/Seiter 1999).

Radio, newspapers, magazines are more intellectual. The most intellectual is said to be the computer, because here no information is accessed without user activity. In contrast, television usage tends to be more passive. Of course, one can argue that TV watching also involves user activity to some extent, but this is mostly manifested in switching TV channels by remote control. Thus, television is a medium of comparatively low interactivity: the user is not allowed to interfere with the content. Although no scholarly studies have concentrated on these issues, there are claims that TV will become an "Entertainment Super Highway" in the same way as networks of computers have turned into "Information Super Highways" (Pavlik 1997). Perhaps future studies will validate these claims. These studies of media uses and misuses will have to clearly define aspects of media usability, that is, which medium is better for what type of information and for what user expectations.

Cognitive psychologists conclude that activity is crucial in the process of learning (Lehtinen et al. 1993). When we are active we are aware of our decision making and we are in control of media exposure. However, much of our exposure is passive which does not result in higher knowledge and deeper insights into the world. Yet, if we accept messages transferred to us by the media unquestioningly, we may end up with faulty beliefs about the world and ourselves.

These faulty beliefs are called naïve claims and some of them are characteristic to interactive media sphere. For example, some time ago it was commonly accepted that new information technologies, i.e. interactive media documents, are simply new means to do old things. This point of view relates to the general growth in multimedia publishing and attempts to transfer conventional publications into interactive electronic versions. The result of such a move is that we have numerous electronic publications that are unusable, unreadable, and simply worthless.

Thus, we suggest that the general call to become multimedia literate applies to both designers and users of interactive multimedia documents. Media literacy not only emphasizes the ability to appreciate messages transferred to us by multimedia, more importantly, it raises awareness for media effects, aims of working with media and the entire process of reading, using, designing contemporary documents.

3.2.2 Media Literacy. A Definition

Generally, media literacy is defined as a perspective from which readers expose themselves to media messages and interpret their meanings (Potter, 1997). To become media literate we need tools and raw material to work with. Tools can be understood as skills and raw material as any type of messages transferred to us by media.

Scholars studying user characteristics tend to define two broad groups of users (cf. Balcytiene 1999b; Petty/Cacioppo 1986; Rouet 1992). The first group is the group having a broad perspective on media effects. Users of this group appreciate messages from various perspectives: cognitive, emotional, moral, and aesthetical. As a result to media exposure this group is able to select one of the above four perspectives and appreciate messages. In contrast, the other group – people operating at a lower degree of media literacy - have a weak and limited perspective on media and their effects. The common feature of people belonging to this group is their inability or unwillingness and, therefore, low motivation to use well-organized schemas to interpret the meaning of media messages.

We as human beings rely on previous experience (which is "stored" in knowledge structures) in making sense of the world. Lack of ability or motivation to take control over one's learning may result in overall disappointment in content. As shown in a study by Balcytiene (1999b), people with lower levels of media literacy are much less capable to identify various meanings of a message and tend to accept the surface meaning in the message itself. Thus, in order to be able to control one's awareness and reactions, it is better to perform at higher degrees of media literacy. Doing so offers the reader many more options to control beliefs and behaviours. Reduced options deliver a closed view of the world with readers accepting the dominant values and beliefs. In our view, this is not what is required from modern readers today. They need to debate.

Media literacy is a continuum. Nóbody was born with the skills one possesses. Acquiring media literacy is a process of constant growth and development. Media literacy is also a multi-dimensional characteristic. Having it, gives more control over one's interpretations.

3.2.3 The Importance of Attitudes in Cognitive Processing of Multimedia Documents. Where does the Reader Motivation Come from?

With multimedia documents, as with any texts, the aspects of cognitive processing are of major importance. One of the recent views to cognitive development emphasizes contextual aspects of learning (Bandura 1994). The effects of context are clearly manifested in understanding that readers acquire. These effects are, again, multi-dimensional – they arise from readers' individual characteristics and from the media being used. User characteristics are described as a complex combination of physiological, sensory, cognitive and socio-cultural factors (Baker 1989). Media characteristics are related to the media (texts, sounds, images) being used.

Cognitive psychologists have emphasized the importance of positive attitudes in learning and education in general. This means that having a positive attitude results in looking, possessing and arriving at conclusions differently than when having a negative attitude. It was observed by many that new instructional media result in positive reactions from learners (Collins et al. 1997; Hakkinen 1996). This affects the learning process positively.

One of the commonly cited models of user engagement is the "Elaboration Likelihood Model" (Petty/Cacioppo 1986). According to this, readers can be engaged by two routes: the central route and the peripheral route. The central route or the "central processing" involves careful thinking about the content of the message, reflecting upon the ideas and information contained in it. This corresponds to a high level of media literacy. The second route is called the peripheral route. The essence of this route is that it involves focusing on so-called peripheral cues of the message such as source attractiveness, quantity of arguments presented, multimedia features and additional effects.

People tend to favour one route over another. Cognitive psychologists suggest that for a person to engage in central processing he/she must have a particular motivation for doing so (Brown 1980). The motivation can be explained as high involvement with the topic or issue. If a person has low involvement, he/she is more likely to use information through peripheral processing.

The "Elaboration Likelihood Model" concludes that the knowledge acquired via the central route tends to be more lasting. This is understandable: if we think and work with concepts the knowledge tends to sink in. Thus, bearing in mind that the interactive environment encourages the reader to take an active role, we can hypothesize that multimedia-based "reading" can be a good environment to stimulate reader's reactions and, therefore, to provoke him/her to take responsibility for their learning. This is emphasized by media education: if readers are active, they interpret media messages, that is, they refer to previous knowledge, they continually question themselves whether they are gaining anything meaningful out of the learning situation. In the end, they become literate.

3.2.4 Promises and Drawbacks of Multimedia

With advances of new (and interactive) media technologies new sets of skills are needed to appreciate various messages transferred by multiple channels. It is commonly understood that messages change if they are transferred from one medium to another. Although each of the media adds its own characteristics to message delivery, there is a generic set of skills which underlies our ability to process any type of media message (Potter 1997).

From what was elaborated earlier we can say that effectiveness of a message is improved if the target of the message – the audience – is actively, cognitively and emotionally involved. Observing the convergence of different types of media we can say that modern multimedia documents (which include numerous texts, images, video clips, impressive sounds, etc.) become documents where users' emotional reaction are most easily achieved. Multimedia scholars claim that multimedia presentations are more attention-getting and attention-holding because they stimulate more than one sense at a time (Collins et al. 1997). Also, it is suggested that multimedia environments can be motivating and engaging because this technology can provide readers with quick and easy access to a wide range of new material.

Although results of those studies are not uniform enough to produce a single, definitive conclusion concerning the relationship between mediated information and attitudes, multimedia allowing an all-inclusive (and, therefore, a democratic) approach is said to have great impacts. But, as recent studies show, media usage does not end with one-sided effects. Taking a closer look at the history of technological inventions one can say that each technology produced a small number of, but very essential drawbacks. ·

Emotional reactions, attained with multimedia, recently became of particular interest and aroused much curiosity. Many designers use emotional reactions as a major stimulant of user's activity. Although one can claim that the multimedia environment is stimulating and, thus, provocative, emotions raised by media draw our attention to the entertaining aspect of multimedia. The demand that learning ought to be fun should not make the entertainment aspect take all the credit in promoting multimedia documents (as it sometimes happens with the new genres "edutainment" and "infotainment").

It is a truism that the multimedia-type of access to information allows readers to interact with information, the negative effects come from the experiential mode of cognition. The experiential mode of cognition involves one with information via the peripheral route. Experiential cognition needs constant excitement by extrinsic stimuli (e.g., a piece of music or attractive visual effects) with one's mind working without much effort and requiring only superficial interaction. One can spend a sufficient amount of time with interactive media and still have the impression that time was wasted. On the one hand, there is nothing wrong with this mode of cognition if the reader is exploring unknown information without any specific goals in mind. Some time is (most certainly) needed for the reader to get a general feel for the document he or she is working with. Only then one is capable to make a core decision whether the document is "readable". On the other hand, studies and scholarly work require deep mental interaction with ideas and concepts. Serious study demands "mirroring", i.e. one refers to past experience (knowledge, attitudes and emotions) and this becomes manifested in decision making and strategic planning. These abilities involve intrinsic motivation and responsibility for one's own learning. Intrinsic motivation comes from within, whereas extrinsic motivation is instilled by some outside factor (Petri 1991).

Although it is claimed that interactive multimedia documents "transfer" readers into an active decision making mode, more and more scholars conclude that observable reader decisions are being made without intrinsic motivation (Balcytiene 1999b). Doubts concerning readers' ability to take responsibility for their own learning also have recently entered scholarly debates (cf. Cameron 1995).

Thus, the question whether deep intellectual study with interactive media is possible needs careful consideration. To shed light on this question, a concrete multimedia document was designed and an empirical study was planned.

3.3   Digital Reflections of Cultural Heritage. "Interactive Excursions to M. K. Ciurlionis' Art"

It is commonly accepted that the advances of new technologies have resulted in greatly expanding opportunities for writers, publishers, and readers. The developments of interactive new media technologies and of online publishing have expanded the chances for users to satisfy their needs in ways undreamed a few years ago.

Recent developments see new media as instrumental for exhibiting cultural heritage. The exhibition of artefacts in museums and artists' lives in new media grows rapidly. There are a number of reasons for this "invasion" of culture by new media, "cultural exhibition" and active participation of audience. Interactive cultural representations are especially fascinating as they free readers of non-linear documents from "hierarchical", i.e. predefined, forms of relationship. The idea behind interactive cultural representations in the new media is that the users (with their background knowledge, temperament and amount of attention paid to the media) become the "centre" and, therefore, invent the order within intertwined nodes of digital information. Some scholars suggest that this organization of cultural content offers a more democratic and, thus, personalized exploration of culture (Balcytiene 1999a; Taylor 1996).

3.3.1   A Modern "Touch" to M.K. Ciurlionis' Abstractions. Some Design Hypotheses.

In Lithuania there has been a startling growth in the use of new media in recent years. Although, the market for Lithuanian new media products is small, it has reached the stage where it is understood that new means offer important ways to explore and comprehend cultural content (Balcytiene 1998). We attempted to go one step further. That is, in our design and case study, multimedia usability effects received particular attention. The questions that we asked in the design process were the following: How do users engage in multimedia? Where does user motivation come from? What do users learn from images? When do they stop explorations?

In order to answer these questions an interactive multimedia document with paintings by Mikalojus K. Ciurlionis was developed. Ciurlionis' works (1875-1911) are well-known in Lithuania as it is described by scholars: "Ciurlionis' life with his work and his presence at times reminds of the phenomena in the sky – the northern lights, a glowing comet, a blinding light of sorts – that come into sight, blind the viewers, and disappear. Whoever saw it, saw it. And those who did not, did not. And those who saw it have a hard time telling others what it was." (Gostautas 1994). In Lithuania no one doubts that Ciurlionis was an extraordinary artist, musician, and painter.

The multimedia application "Interactive Excursions to M. K. Ciurlionis' Art" was designed for experimental purposes. The process of designing and working with images and texts has proved that this kind of content – paintings of Ciurlionis – fits nicely into contemporary interactive multimedia design. The two-dimensional collection was created with *Macromedia Director* (in the future even some three-dimensional interfaces of the artist's paintings seem possible).

The multimedia document – an interactive net of Ciurlionis' paintings – contains over 200 paintings that were scanned and converted into two-dimensional images. Originally, many of Ciurlionis' paintings had no titles or the titles changed with political tides. Thus, only paintings with clear titles were included.

The hypothesis of introducing and structuring visual information in a multimedia application was to stimulate reader's understanding of symbols and, thus, to develop an ability to critically "read" Ciurlionis' paintings. For this purpose an ever-changing collection of images is presented to the reader as an interactive network. The idea of implementing images into the network was realized by an experienced art critic specialized in Ciurlionis' painting and his symbolism. The entire design process can be retold in the following way: the art critic "selected" several symbols on each of the 200 paintings and attempted to "decode" each symbol's meaning. It is important to notice that only symbols that are clearly visible and are easy to "pick up" were selected as "active symbols". These particular symbols were indicated to the reader through a specific change in the pointer of the mouse – whenever the user positions the mouse over the corresponding symbol, the pointer changes indicating that further exploration in this direction is possible. It was hoped that this would catch the reader's attention and stimulate him/her to further analysis.

Ciurlionis' paintings are "saturated" with symbols. It is said that Ciurlionis was the first abstract painter of modern times. The painter used hundreds of complex symbols that acquire different meanings in different contexts. For example, the symbol "angel" can induce complex meanings, e.g. either create hope or, in the case of the "dark angel", indicate loss. The symbol "sun" also creates numerous feelings: warmth, change, hope, lightness, etc.

There are 574 electronic links in the program. The average of linked symbols in one particular painting is 5.22. This number was selected on purpose, as, according to contemporary studies, users are able to work with 5 (plus/minus 2) different units of information and experience no cognitive overload or any other similar kind of discomfort.

3.3.2   About the Reading Process

The user enters the program through the image, i.e. painting, called "Rex". This particular painting offers the highest number of symbols and this was a valid reason to have it as the main entrance.

On the computer screen the user can see the painting and a small "guiding map" with links to other images to his/her right. It was hoped that the user would investigate the painting, i.e. the connections that are available and would make up his/her mind on what direction to follow. This process resembles strategic decision making of one coming to a crossroad.

The navigation mechanism is quite simple: The user is allowed to "backtrack" (through the "back" sign) to the previous image or to move forward to a new image (through any of the symbols that are active). Although it is claimed that multimedia documents are interactive, we would call our document as having a fairly low level of interactivity.

The entire process of "reading" such a document relies on several factors: on previous knowledge, on reader's intuition, on screen elements that attract reader's attention and so forth. Some similarities with another cultural form – hyperfiction – can be seen. With hyperfiction, however, the reader has no further vision of where he/she is going and has to rely only upon information that he/she gets on the screen. In our case, it is hoped that every symbol "suggests" the mood of the preceding painting. And if this mood conflicts with user's expectations, he/she can select another route or come back to the previous image and think again.

We had several goals that are manifested in the digital design of the document. First, we tried to provoke the reader to think carefully about the relationships among paintings and the meanings of symbols. Through this particular goal – to make the reader an active thinker – another important design aspect reveals itself: We were very much attracted to the ideas of constructivism and we wanted to test the cognitive abilities of any particular reader. That is, for our purpose, we wanted to have an experimental hypertext-based document with a fairly flexible usage mechanism.

Flexibility, democratic access, frankness are used as claims in the promotion of digital documents. The multimedia product used in this study had no pre-defined way of usage (except for the starting point, the "Rex"). Suggestions or recommendations of content experts (art critics, teachers, media experts etc.) were not included. The reader was left on his/her own. The only additional texts that were visible on the computer screen were the title, a list of techniques of painting (tempera, pencil, ink etc.) and the year of creation of the work of art in question.

3.3.3 About Hands-on Experience. Concrete Case Study as a Foreground for further Debate

The main hypothesis of the study is that users will investigate the collection of images and, therefore, will create their personalized experiences of Ciurlionis' way of painting and his works of art.

The empirical part of the study was designed to evaluate both the students' background knowledge and their awareness of their characteristics as learners. For this particular goal a specific question was generated to estimate (using scales from 1 to 7) their ability to recognize whether the art work was a painting of Ciurlionis or not.

The subjects of the study were 15 students of Journalism from the Graduate School of Journalism at Vytautas Magnus University in Kaunas. The students had diverse backgrounds – with basic degrees in Catholic theology (2), history (3), arts (2), foreign languages (5), political science (2), management (1). The average age of the participants was 24.6 years.

According to the pre-test result, when student's awareness of Ciurlionis' way of painting was estimated, students assessed themselves as fairly experienced evaluators able to recognize the painter's art work. The average estimation was 5.53 out of 10. Students could also prove their knowledge by either remembering titles of concrete paintings or by being able to retell the general mood that was created through symbols. The pre-test results show that Journalism students envisage themselves as knowledgeable subjects who possess knowledge on both content and learning abilities.

All the participants were required to use the multimedia document with a general aim – "to get a feeling of the multimedia document and its content". Students were informed that they will be required to fill in a post-test questionnaire and talk about their feelings, impressions and attitudes towards the particular design and content.

3.4 Discussion. Problems will not "Kill" Enthusiasm

Although the case study was designed to evaluate the document's usability issues and to assess the "reading" process, it disclosed several aspects that need careful consideration before proceeding any further. We also paid attention to the following issues, first overlooked:

- The conflict between narrative models offered in traditional media and new media interactivity. This conflict is understood as a continuous debate on the roles that reader and author must undertake.
- The different modes of working with multimedia: experiential, which is mostly associated with fun and careless wandering in interactive

documents, and reflective, which is a version of deep academic study required in building knowledge structures.

3.4.1   Interactivity as a Unique Feature of Modern Media. Promises and Drawbacks

Interactivity of new media documents is usually stressed as a unique and, therefore, very desirable feature (Pavlik 1997; Fidler 1997). However, in most of these claims understanding of what constitutes a good interactive design is usually overlooked. It is quite common that authors and designers of interactive documents emphasize readers' preferences for a very flexible contact with multimedia documents forgetting about one core question: Whether this interactivity is exactly what is needed in the particular case. It is quite common that a designer has a naïve conception of user/reader and provides him/her with a raw material to be applied in further explorations.

In our case, we will concentrate on the importance of schemas (i.e. mental models or knowledge structures acquired through experience) in making decisions on a document's usability. We will also stress some similarities of our document to hyperfiction.

Cognitive aspects of (new) media usage. Schemas and the process of making inferences

In everyday life users expose themselves to numerous texts which, according to cognitive theorists, lead readers to acquire mental models or schemas for documents with which they become familiar. Previous research (for example, on text comprehension) has clearly demonstrated the complexity of the cognitive processing that occurs whenever readers expose themselves to new documents and unexperienced situations (Anderson 1983; Kintsch 1974).

Cognitive psychologists use the word schema to refer to a kind of mental template which is used to provide powerful organizing principles for information. Schemas are used when we interpret our experiences. From our everyday experience with documents we can understand the importance of our expectations in making sense of new experiences. For example, when we pick up a book we immediately have expectations on its age, contents, amount and quality of information presented. Experienced users know all this before even exposing themselves to the content of any document. According to contemporary schema theory, interpreting events involves mapping the available information onto an appropriate schema which is already stored in memory (Anderson 1983). This applies whether the situation involves buying something in a shop, reading a story, watching TV, entering a restaurant and so forth. We derive all these schemas from our past experience and spontaneously apply them in new situations.

The most important aspect of schemas, however, is that schemas also set up expectances about the contents of any document, what media are being used there, how information is grouped etc. Although, at the very beginning, readers can tell little about the content, the general knowledge and expectations of a document's organisational structure supplies stability, orientation and safety. For example, we all know how to read newspapers and what kind of information to expect there; we have expectations of media that can be used with printed documents (texts and images); we have expectations of story structures and genres that are used in news writing.

In contrast, the concept of schema in an electronic information space is practically non-defined, which is not surprising as electronic documents do not have that long a history as equivalents in traditional media. Most importantly, this is due to the fact that electronic documents do not provide much "transparency".

"Convergence", the buzzword in contemporary media, might offer some insights into the problem. "Convergence" does not only mean general change and interchange of print, broadcast and computers. It also means that many genres and many media are applicable within digital documents (Fidler 1997). Although this applicability allows more freedom and creativity for both users and designers, this adds an enormous amount of cognitive requirements. According to Dillon (1994), once the reader looses knowledge of how big the entire document is, how many and what quality texts and images are included, other factors come into play. At this stage readers must manipulate documents and be able to relate current to previously displayed material.

In studying user characteristics, it is important to remember that users are not consciously aware of the process of applying schemas when they are exposed to documents. It is more apparent when a text disrupts user expectations. We, as human beings, seek pleasure and seek to avoid pain in every situation. That is, we seek to profit from each situation and avoid loss. Although the challenge offered by interactive media can be appreciated by some, such as perhaps lovers of avant-garde, for others such disruptions can be irritating and confusing.

Hyperfiction and beyond. Similarities with game playing

The experimental condition revealed some similarities of the "interactive net" of Ciurlionis' paintings to interactive literature. The main characteristic of hyperfiction is the new, non-linear, non-sequential form of reading (and writing). It is said that hyperfiction is the form of writing in which the author creates characters, environments and motivation, but no predetermined plot. If there is no plot, this means that there is no clear argumentative structure. Thus, there is no clearly defined end.

What disappears in hyperfiction is the notion of a single narrative line, not narrativity itself. Stories are still being read, but the user is both reader and original creator. It is claimed that interactivity promotes motivation and desires to reach the end and to achieve resolution. However, it does not fulfil this desire in the end. Interactivity promotes some version of freedom, however, in the long run this freedom might turn into meaningless wandering. Thus, tension grows and becomes an inherent feature to the reading process. Although the mechanism of hypertext is associative and it promotes freedom to make desirable associations, the users find themselves in quite a different situation. With hypertext each node turns into a crossroad where the reader is required to make a decision which way to follow next. Although this involves user activity, in the long run this task turns into a cognitively unbearable requirement for the reader. Previous experience suggests the narrative model of information: there is always a beginning, development and resolution. Although with information some wandering is allowed, it is always hoped that any wandering will lead to satisfaction (in the form of resolution) and that not much of new information is left outside as unchecked, unvisited, unread, unexplored.

It can be assumed that due to interactivity new media usage shares characteristics with game playing (Balcytiene 1999c). Momentary reaction, spontaneous construction of meaning, unexpectedness in results are typical characteristics of any game. But games have rules that are clear to a player. With hyperfiction (or with any hypertext), the reader is confused, he/she sees the "game", but has little idea of what the rules for that particular "game" are. In other words, with interactive designs the reader has no information of what connections are possible, what arguments are behind the connections, who has added a specific structure into this document and why and for what purpose. As a result the reader clicks around in a rather chaotic and unmotivated way. Thus, interactive media stimulate experiential learning with actions activated by spontaneous reaction to the image that appears on the computer screen.

Amidst duty and hedonism

Interactive media are an anxious environment and one that contains an illusionary call for a wish-fulfilment (cf. Cameron 1995). Many claim that multimedia creates an attractive, engaging and alluring environment. However, if we want multimedia documents to enter other areas of our life (not only the ones associated with temporary exploration), we need to take a closer look at successful communications principles.

What is overlooked in most interactive designs is the notion that any successful communication requires skilled and talented authors who bring up (in one way or another) predictable end results. Successful communication conveys information on core elements. Journalism and news writing lessons could be easily applied here, as every communicative situation contains the who, what, where, when, why and how of description. Moreover, these descriptions also convey value judgements.

Our minds are made of schemas, organized into stories in which elements are invested with value and emotions. What makes a story interesting is the storyteller who brings up what he/she thinks as valuable in the story. The multimedia environment transfers this responsibility to the readers as they have to draw the conclusions for themselves. But then the problems arise: What happens if the reader has no ability or motivation to engage into continuous debate with himself/herself? The answer may simply be that he/she attempts to escape that kind of experience.

Although interactivity promotes freedom, this might just be an illusion. A non-linear construction of meaning becomes a cognitively unbearable task for the reader. Even though the illusion is there, the resolution and fulfilment is never attained. The reader is tempted to check the document with a continuous question: Will I be lucky this time and will I achieve a desirable resolution?" Although disappointment might be there, the reader has no time to indulge into it as he/she is already being "provoked" by another stimulant on the screen. Due to the interactive nature the reader is being put into a temporary study mode and struggles with duty (i.e. requirements to reach resolution) and multimedia features (that create an emotionally rich and, thus, fascinating environment).

3.4.2   The Confession. New Publishing Models are Required

The new media environment gives and takes away. Sometimes new technologies create more than they destroy. Sometimes they destroy more than they create. But the effects are never one-sided.

So far, scholarly studies have concentrated on gains and overlooked losses. One major conclusion becoming apparent in our case study is that interactivity requires users to recognize what they can and cannot do with the new technology. The understanding of this provides issues for further investigations.

It is widely acknowledged that the new media mechanism is associative (Bush 1945; Nelson 1990). It is truism that associative data models do not constrain the relationships as much as rule-based engines. Thus, it becomes much easier to extract information: once rich domain knowledge exists, it can be combined in many ways. For example, new media allows one to explore paintings of Ciurlionis in radically new ways. By activating symbols from the painting (which can currently be seen on the screen) the user can obtain an ever-changing collection of artefacts. So far, the only way and form of studying Ciurlionis' paintings was the classification of the paintings into several periods and, then, describing each period in a time line. Multimedia provides an obvious gain: With the help of interactive media one gets an excellent opportunity to explore Ciurlionis' paintings in a way that is unreachable by hitherto used means.

Although it sounds obvious, practice shows that this way of "reading" and understanding requires an enormous reorganization of human knowledge. Contemporary studies conclude that many factors influence human reactions, among which are the physiological, sensory/motor, cognitive, and cultural factors. Therefore, taking these factors into consideration, writers and readers should understand that the new digital medium is not an optimal interface for detailed cultural research. Physiological experiments show that users see a third less when light comes to the eye directly from the computer screen rather than from printed page (Dillon 1994). And this physiological factor is crucial with digital documents.

Although the process of getting to know content might resemble browsing, careful studies suggest that some essential characteristics of human behaviour might provide additional insight. Most importantly, these findings suggest that a reader does not simply "scan" information. Instead, he/she enters a document through a single element which is the most vividly exposed (cf. Garcia 1997). In the act of reading the eye of the experienced reader does not simply start at the beginning of a text and proceed from word to word until it reaches the end, instead it jumps across the page as the mind searches for organizing patterns which make the task of reading easier (cf. Just and Carpenter 1980).

We are always relying on our past experiences to guide the ways in which we interpret our present experiences. Another drawback is the estimation of length of information. Human factors specialists stress that digital media do not provide readers with essential knowledge on the length of information or how many illustrations are included in digital texts and so forth (cf. Dillon 1994). Physical books provide readers with information as to length, size, year of publication, etc. As a result of dealing with print media, readers have acquired some basic models of how to read and comprehend messages conveyed by basic types of printed documents (e.g., by conventional newspapers, books, magazines, brochures, etc.). The electronic equivalents also need to convey the characteristics essential for human cognition. Therefore, some authors introduce a three-dimensional conceptual space as a solution to provide readers with at least some information on what knowledge (and how much of it) is exhibited in the new media (Balcytiene 1999a).

Many writers have overlooked the fact that, although associations might seem meaningful, in many cases (due to the lack of background information on how the nodes are related to each other) the reader might experience discomfort. This is called a deficit in background knowledge. It shows that selections users make are subjective: a reader leans on his/her experience to interpret any new situation. If he/she sees no relevance for association, the reading process turns into meaningless wandering.

We, therefore, suggest that mere employment of electronic links does not produce desirable effects. The interactive medium is far from being a flexible and democratic medium. In order to develop into such a medium, the reader has to become a so-called hyper-reader who possesses the ability of being multimedia-literate. This means that he/she possesses an understanding of how messages are constructed and transferred through multimedia. Only then, we can expect the new media to open up other (significant) areas of our life.

Many multimedia designs can be seen as competing for reader's attention on how impressive, provocative or in other ways challenging the whole exploration can become. Feelings provoked by new media are typical of our times – being a period of no fixed beliefs, no commitments and uncertain standards. Our times are characterised by relaxation, hedonism, individualism, living in the present moment (cf. Taylor 1993). These aspects are manifested in interactive multimedia designs: we continually search for novelty and invention, we seek momentary reaction and enjoyment, we dream of euphoria, nostalgia, playfulness. As the fixed goal disappears, the major aim of the designers becomes to create more opportunities for fun and enjoyment.

3.5   Synthesis. Where Shall We Go Now?

From what has been said, it becomes clear that new technology brings positive and negative elements into the process of reading electronic documents. Content exposure suffers. Search for new publishing models is a gain. The new means also offer different possibilities for appreciation and criticism. The issues concerning human engagement in technology and multimedia persuasion need careful consideration and have to be addressed before creating versions of digital culture.

Achieving defined knowledge shouldn't be a goal of working with new interactive media. Results from contemporary studies show that interactive documents are better suited for temporary exploration rather than for long and intensive study. Concerning our design, interactive exposure of Ciurlionis' paintings is not useless. On the contrary, it is a significant new way to get a modern "touch" to what is understood and valued as cultural heritage. The new approach expands the aura of the Master and his heritage.

From what we have seen (students working with the multimedia document) and heard (students talking about their attitudes and impressions) we were encouraged to design a new version of a multimedia document. For this version, one painting of the entire collection (from over 200 scanned images) will be randomly offered to the students, thus, allowing them to create their own "nets" through associations. There will be no restrictions as to when exactly the reader should finish explorations. Moreover, the readers will be free to select as many symbols on any painting as they consider important. All the steps the reader makes will be recorded. This should enable us to find out about relations of the net's complexity to reader's characteristics (involvement, motivation etc.).

The paradox of our times is that we build more computers to hold information, to produce more copies than ever, but have less communication. We write more, but learn less. We plan more, but accomplish less. It seems to be time to acknowledge that we live in times where there is much in the "show window", but little in the content. It is true, we have new and very powerful means to distribute information but we must also understand that any text without an able reader is useless.

Although computers remove barriers of storage capacity, new challenges require attention from both writers and users of multimedia documents. The challenge of scholars may lie less in conveying facts than in teaching users to look at facts and concepts in new ways both experienced with traditional media and not imagined before. Although the "translations" of physical into virtual space constitute the most obvious application of the new media technologies, for the communications field the most exciting challenge might be to see user reactions.

We attempted to get a feeling of what characteristics of multimedia documents restrict broader acknowledgement of these documents. Some people are more capable of cognitive processing than others. Whether multimedia environment is comfortable, relaxing and stimulating for readers to take responsibility for what they gain is a question for further empirical study.

We acknowledge that to fully enjoy and appreciate the challenge and provocation offered by interactive multimedia design the user must be either a sincere avant-garde lover or an experienced learner. In both cases, he/she must have the ability to continually debate and question the process of "reading". This ability is described as general self-awareness, self-regulation, or intentional learning, which from the point of view of cognitive psychology is qualified as meta-cognition (cf. Balcytiene 1999b; Brown 1980; Rouet 1992). From the communications perspective, this ability is qualified as literacy (Potter 1997).

It is not enough to require users to read and use digital documents. It is not enough to tell that readers must take risks and be open for further explorations. Most important is the acknowledgement that the reader must be inherently motivated to challenge himself/herself with new situations to learn, unlearn and re-learn. The reader is the key. Awareness of his/her characteristics will empower us to design usable multimedia.

3.6 References

Anderson, J. 1983. *The Architecture of Cognition*. Cambridge, MA: Harvard University Press.

Baker, W. 1989. "Human Factors, Ergonomics and Usability: Principles and Practice". In: E. Klemmer (ed.). *Ergonomics: Harness the Power of Human Factors in your Business*. Norwood: Ablex Publishing Comp.

Balcytiene, A. 1998. *Digital reflections of cultural heritage*. [in Lithuanian: *Kompiuteriniai kulturos paveldo pavyzdziai*] Istoria. Vol. 27.

Balcytiene, A. 1999a. "Cultural Representation in the New Media". *Lituanus* 45.4.

Balcytiene, A. 1999b. *Exploring Individual Processes in Knowledge Construction with Hypertext. Instructional Science*.

Balcytiene, A. 1999c. *Beyond the Suggestions of New Media Interactivity*. [in Lithuanian] Online: http://www.artium.lt

Bandura, A. 1994. "Social cognitive theory of mass communication". In: J. Bryant/D. Zillman (eds.). *Media Effects: Advances in Theory and Research*. Hillsdale, NJ: Lawrence Erlbaum Associates. 61-89.

Brown, A. 1980. "Metacognitive development in reading". In: R. Spiro/B. Bruce/W. Brewer (eds.). *Theoretical Issues in Reading Comprehension*. Hillsdale, NJ: Lawrence Erlbaum Associates. 453-481.

Bush, V. 1945. *As we may think*. Online: http://www.ps.uni-sb.de/~duchier/pub/vbush/vbush.html

Cameron, A. 1995. *Dissimulations: Illusions of Interactivity*. Online: http://www.wmin.ac.uk/media/VD/Dissimulations.html

Collins, J./M. Hammond/J. Wellington. 1997. *Teaching and Learning with Multimedia*. London: Routledge.

Dillon, A. 1994. *Designing Usable Electronic Text*. London: Taylor & Francis.

Fidler, R. 1997. *Mediamorphosis: Understanding New Media*. London: Pine Forge Press.

Garcia, M. 1997. *Redesigning Print for the Web*. Hayden Books.

Gass, R./J. Seiter. 1999. *Persuasion, Social Influence, and Compliance Gaining*. Boston: Allyn and Bacon.

Gostautas, S. 1994. *Ciurlionis: Painter and Composer*. Vilnius: Vaga.

Hakkinen, P. 1996. *Design, take into sue and effects of computer-based learning environments*. PhD Theses. University of Joensuu, Finland.

Just, M./P. Carpenter, P. 1980. *A Theory of Reading: From Eye Movements to Comprehension*. In: *Psychological Review* 87/4. 329-354.

Kintsch, W. 1974. *The Representation of Meaning in Memory*. Hillsdale, NJ: Lawrence Erlbaum Associates.

Landauer, T. 1997. *The Trouble with Computers*. London: MIT Press.

Lehtinen, E./A. Balcytiene/M. Gustafson. 1993. *Designing Hypertext-Based Learning Environment: An Activity-Oriented Approach.* Paper presented at 5th EARLI conference in Aix-en-Provence.

Nelson, T. 1990. *Literary Machines.* Sausalito, CA: Mindful Press.

Pavlik, J. 1997. *New Media Technology: Cultural and Commercial Perspectives.* Boston: Allyn and Bacon.

Petri, H. 1991. *Motivation Theory: Research and Application.* Belmont, CA: Wadsworth.

Petty, R./J. Cacioppo, J. 1986. *Communication and Persuasion: Central and Peripheral Routes to Attitude Change.* New York: Springer.

Potter, W. J. 1997. *Media Literacy.* London: Sage Publications.

Rouet, J.-F. 1992. "Cognitive processing of hyper-documents. When does non-linearity help?". In: *Proceedings of the ACM Conference on Hypertext, Milano.* 131-140.

Taylor, J. 1993. "Learning in the non-linear world: a critical postmodernist reading." In: *Proceedings of Conference on Computers and Hypermedia in Education: Hypermedia in Vaaasa 1993.* 266-273.

Taylor, J. 1996. "New Media and Cultural Representation." In: K. Gill (ed.). *Information Society: Media, Ethics and Postmodernism.* New York: Springer.

4 Interactive TV. Planned Educational Uses versus Real Educational Needs
Stuart Nolan, UK

Interactive TV technologies have the potential to facilitate new methods of providing learning experiences to the home and the workplace. Many more digital channels can be broadcast than previously possible with analogue systems. Programmes will be cheaper to produce and broadcast and the user will be able to interact in a number of novel ways. Interactivity can be of great importance in the distance learning systems.

The combination of low cost and interactivity makes Interactive TV an interesting avenue for educationalists and governments who need to find new Fordian systems for providing the increasing global and local demand for learning.

4.1 Globalisation of Education and the Changing Need for Learning

How does the globalisation of the economy affect the nature of education? The early developers of global education show considerable unanimity about the curriculum areas which define current trends: MBAs and business studies, information technology and computer-related subjects, and open and distance education qualifications with languages and cultural subjects forming a smaller, but growing area. These topics reflect the demands of a lifelong learning market that currently centres on professional updating, IT skilling and, to a lesser extent, leisure concerns.

Mason (1998) observes a number of trends:

- a movement away from simple broadcast or satellite TV as a means to deliver course content;
- a move towards interactivity and communication between participants;
- a trend towards joint course development;
- a trend towards individualised learning;
- a trend towards online support systems.

Additionally, Mason (1998) predicts that:

> The increasing diversity of educational opportunities represented by digital TV and the Web will lead to the growth of a new educational role: a sort of super-tutor who knows what resources, courses, and information sources are available in a particular area, and helps the average citizen navigate through networks, identifying the materials worth attending to and those to ignore, recommending a personal learning plan […]. Just as people have personal fitness trainers, so they will have personal learning trainers.

So, the question I will deal with is: How can Interactive TV assist in providing information for and about learning?

As the world moves towards greater and cheaper electronic communications capacity, trade and investment flows are transforming patterns of economic activity around the world (cf. Cairncross 1998). In a world where communications cost practically nothing and the trend is towards service industries, services can be produced at a distance and the jobs can move to the people.

Global marketing allows companies to trade many services anywhere in the world and countries with skilled, flexible labour forces and relatively low wage costs will succeed. Bangalore, for example, has a flourishing software industry exporting "remote maintenance" services to the US.[1] Nearer home, Ireland is becoming a prime site for call centres in Europe (cf. Murray 1997).

America's output, measured in tons, remains about as heavy as it was a century ago, yet its real GDP in value is twenty times greater. This shift is due to the rising proportion of "knowledge" content of goods and services.[2] America's stock of intangible investment overtook its stock of physical investment during the 1980s. Knowledge is becoming the primary commodity.

Not only is the importance of knowledge growing quickly, the time lag between discovery and application – the information "float" – is rapidly shrinking. It is estimated that Americans currently have to re-train 3 to 4 times within their working lives and that educational bodies will have less time to plan for jobs that don't exist yet (Thornburg 2000).

There are a number of factors that drive the need for effective distance learning systems; many of them also tie in with UK University for Industry (UFI) aims discussed later:

- the expense of higher education needed to compete in a global service led market;
- the increase in the need for lifelong learning;
- the need to skill and re-skill those with little access to current forms of education;
- the opportunity to develop bonds between global peers, which allows economic training of minority interest groups.

---

[1] Cf. "Bangalore Bytes". *The Economist*, 23 March 1996.
[2] Cf. Alan Greenspan, Chairman of the Federal Reserve Board. Quoted in: Cairncross (1998).

It has been argued (Nipper, 1989; Kaufman, 1989) that there are three generations of distance education:

- the first generation predominantly uses a single technology;
- the second generation has a deliberately integrated multiple media approach;
- the third generation may use many media types but is based on two-way communications media that allow for direct interaction between the tutors, facilitators, administrators and students.

The generations progressively allow for more learner control, opportunities for dialogue and emphasis on thinking skills rather than mere comprehension.

Interactive TV systems can provide the two-way communications technology necessary to develop third generation learning systems if guided correctly. However, the danger at present is that the emphasis will be overly based on content provision rather than on system provision.

4.2 Research Aims, Scope and Method

The initial research proposal began with the following statement: "When developing complex learning institutions and systems there are many pitfalls connected with 'choice of technology'. Past mistakes have shown that it is hard to know which technologies to use when confronted with a large range of competing systems in a commercial arena that allows few survivors."

The project aimed to establish key technologies, systems and procedures for the continued development of effective learning technologies by taking two complimentary approaches: (1) a technology survey, and (2) a study of expert opinion. Both approaches have progressed and adapted to suit the modified aims of the research.

The original aim of the research can be broadly described thus: "To inform educational bodies of the Interactive TV technologies and industry in order that these bodies may take informed decisions regarding their involvement in this area." This has been modified to add the following aim: "To inform the Interactive TV industry of the needs of educational bodies."

This change has come about through a realisation that the act of interviewing industry executives and questioning their approaches to education was unavoidably influencing their thinking and that this influence was generally positive.

4.2.1   Why Commercial, Mass Market Interactive TV?

The Interactive TV industry is very broad and the term "Interactive TV" can be applied to a number of widely different services. It is neither the intention of this research to attempt a definition of what Interactive TV is, will be or should be nor will we attempt an exhaustive overview of the field.

The research topic has been limited to commercial, mass market Interactive TV. This choice reflects the belief that the future of Interactive TV use in education will be guided by the systems produced for the commercial arena and that these systems will be designed for a mass market.

Defining the topic in this way allows several systems that may not at first be obvious as Interactive TV systems to be considered. The most exotic of these are the next generation of game consoles that allow Internet access, albeit of a limited nature, through the TV set. The notion of using a game console to access Web-based educational material may seem ironic and fanciful, but many Interactive TV executives see the consoles as a threat to the digital TV set top box. Steve Billinger, Director of Programming at Sky TV has stated that "[...] the next generation game consoles are in the Internet TV market."[3]

Jacobs/Dransfield (1998) give six reasons why prediction of development of the Interactive TV market is problematic and I expand on them here:

(1) Interactive TV is not a single new technology but an amalgam of existing and developing technologies, which complicates prediction.

(2) The extent to which the very passivity of present day TV is its main attraction is difficult to assess. The problem is that we don't know how much the public want to interact, and in what ways, until they have been given the chance.

(3) The extent to which the public will pay for services is difficult to predict, especially when they are used to free-to-air TV and many free services on the Internet.

(4) There are a number of unresolved technical problems with Interactive TV. The lack of a standard being at the centre of most of these.

(5) Broadcast TV is traditionally national in character and in technical delivery. Again the incompatibility of deliberately or accidentally fragmented markets may slow progress.

(6) TV viewing has generally been a group or family activity based on entertainment, whereas many Interactive TV services are predominantly solitary and task-based.

---

[3] Steve Billinger speaking at "Remote Control: Commissioning Content for Interactive TV", the first BAFTA event on the topic of Interactive TV; 21 June 1999.

All these factors make the Interactive TV market difficult to predict, as forecaster's inconsistent attempts to quantify the expected value show. This research has been designed to avoid the pitfalls of prediction by seeking consensus from a selected panel of experts, using a technology survey and a Delphi study of expert opinion. The research will accumulate information rather than solve specific practical problems.

4.2.2 Survey in the Technology

The technology survey will isolate the general enablements that are appearing in Interactive TV development and categorise them in terms of functionality rather than by differences in underlying technological architecture. It may be desirable, however, to comment on any technologies that are using non-standard or out-dated components as these may prove to have a short functional lifespan.

The technology survey delivers an overview of the current technologies and a comparison of their potential usefulness in learning. The areas of technology considered cover:

- Interactive TV delivery systems;
- Interactive TV-related database and tracking systems;
- Interactive TV content production technologies.

Leaders of the field have proposed issues that should receive priority in Open and Distance Learning research (Dalkey 1995; Bates 1995). Hawkridge (1995, 85) proposed a "draft agenda for evaluation of distance education" that identified three key areas: course content, media choice, and student support.

While media choice is the main target of this research the potential effects on course content and student support will be considered. Due to both the complexities of predicting the Interactive TV market already described and the specifically educational nature of the research, an extension of a methodology designed specifically to appraise educational technology has been developed.

Bates (1991; 1995) developed the agenda for research in the area of media choice:

- Where will students learn if they use this technology, at home, at work, in local centres?
- What are the costs, capital and recurrent, fixed and variable?
- What are the presentational requirements of the subject?
- Do students and teachers require a great deal of training to use the technology?
- What changes in organisation will be required to facilitate the use of a particular technology?

- To what extent will the 'trendiness' of this technology stimulate funding and innovation?
- How quickly can new courses be developed using this technology?
- How quickly and easily can material in this technology be updated?

These questions provide guidelines for the technology survey but, depending on the nature of the technology under review, each question will be more or less relevant. To the questions proposed by Bates I add the general questions:

- How can this technology help to stimulate and sustain a demand for learning?
- How can this technology be used to support existing learners?
- How can this technology support the administration of education?

It must be borne in mind that an analysis of the sort Bates proposes is only possible when a specific use in a specific context is being considered. In this research judgements will be broader and certain specifics, such as cost and effect on organisation, will be difficult to assess.

4.2.3 Studying Expert Opinion

The technology survey provides the foundation material for the Delphi study questions. The Delphi method is heavily reliant upon the proper selection of an expert panel (cf. Dalkey 1969; Stackman 1974). Experts are being selected on the basis of recognised involvement with programs utilising new Interactive TV technologies. They will be drawn from: content providers, analysts, technology developers, service carriers, and broadcasters. Consensus of opinion will be sought in order to build on the knowledge base of the technology survey and identify general trends in the technology industries under review.

Schnaars (1989) has warned of the dangers of using mathematical analysis in forecasting and the dangers are exacerbated in a technological environment. With this in mind it was decided that a qualitative forecasting technique would be more appropriate.

It has been shown that the Interactive TV market is dominated by a small number of private media giants which control the industry and whose decisions impact disproportionately on its future (Jacobs/Dransfeld, 1998). A qualitative forecasting method of the expert knowledge variety such as the Delphi method was therefore deemed appropriate.

This paper reports on the interviews for the Delphi study panel. Interviews and questionnaires were examined for models of the social worlds that are implicit in the texts and for clues to the framework within which the interviewee is operating. The epistemological, conceptual foundation for this research was based on a qualitative–illuminative paradigm. The work was undertaken from a constructivist perspective regarding the social and historical context of the survey sample as important in the process of analysis.

All in all, 42 company executives were interviewed. These were selected from companies with known interests in Interactive TV. Individuals were selected by prominence within the Interactive TV field and by seniority within the company. It may be argued that seemingly prominent individuals may not necessarily be those with influence.

Although the interviews were kept informal a number of specific topics were raised within each. As the aim is to look at industry views in relation to the use of technology as an educational tool it was decided to base the preliminary interviews on the same questions, derived from Bates, as asked in the technology survey. To this questions based on the main current Distance Learning initiatives of the UK government were added. The next section looks at the stated aims of these initiatives.

4.3   Interactive TV and the UK Government

> Across the spectrum of working life there is a continuing decline in demand for unskilled labour. This is coupled with increases in the number of service, managerial and professional jobs, and rising skills demands across occupations as a whole. To stay competitive and prosperous, the UK needs a culture of lifelong learning among adults of all ages and in all occupations.

This quote of the UK Government indicates that the Government recognises the need for a lifelong learning system and has set out a number of initiatives in order to improve lifelong learning provision. Central to these initiatives are the *University for Industry* (UfI) and the *National Grid for Learning*. I will consider the potential role of Interactive TV in these two initiatives and comments on the potential of Interactive TV.

In order to consider the role of Interactive TV in UfI plans I will consider the stated objectives of the UfI one by one:[4]

UfI will have two strategic objectives: (1) to stimulate demand for lifelong learning amongst businesses and individuals; and (2) to promote the availability of, and improve access to, relevant, high quality and innovative learning, in particular through the use of information and communications technologies.

In meeting these objectives, the UfI will help overcome the barriers which deter people and businesses – in particular smaller firms – from learning, by:

---

[4] Cf. University for Industry (UfI). *Pathfinder Prospectus*. Parts 1.2 and 1.3.

- "[...] harnessing technologies to make learning provision more flexible: The UfI will help people find the time to learn." Harnessing existing technology and infrastructure will reduce costs and allow learning systems to integrate naturally and unobtrusively into the home. Learning from home allows flexible study and helps put learners in control of their learning.

- "[...] stimulating new learning markets: The UfI will help bring costs down and make learning more accessible and affordable." Managed correctly Interactive TV systems could become a low cost way of providing information about learning opportunities to the home. Advertisements for learning could stimulate new markets.

- "[...] offering reliable and accessible information and advice: The UfI will provide a clear route to learning opportunities." New TV systems such as digital teletext can provide up-to-date, easy to use information. Access to e-mail via TV can connect learners to sources of advice and directions to learning opportunities.

- "[...] allowing people to learn at their own pace, in a familiar, convenient and supportive environment: The UfI will take the fear out of learning." This is clearly talking about learning from home. Added support can be provided through e-mail.

The concentration on new communications technologies and individuals and small businesses shows that the Government is aware of the general trend towards a fractured, flexible workforce that we have previously considered. Working and studying from home may be facilitated by new TV-based systems.

The Government has stated that "network literacy is already an important skill in the workplace. Increasingly it will become an essential requirement for study and for work."[5] Network literacy is usually interpreted to mean PC network skills, but while these are necessary, there are other ways to access information networks.

The Government has laid out the aims of a network, the *National Grid for Learning*, to serve its planned learning society and summarises them thus as follows:[6]

- teachers will be able to share and discuss best practice with each other and with experts while remaining in their schools;

- materials and advice will be available online – when learners want them – to help develop their literacy and numeracy skills;

- children in isolated schools will be able to link up with their counterparts' curriculum, to help them to work together and gain the stimulus they need;

---

[5] Cf. *Open for Learning, Open for Business*. Point 12. *National Grid for Learning*. Online: http://www.ngfl.gov.uk

[6] Cf. *Connecting the Learning Society*. The Government's consultation paper on the National Grid for Learning. Online: http://www.dfee.gov.uk/grid/consult/index.htm

- language learners will be able to communicate directly with speakers of the target language;
- learners at home or in libraries will be able to access a wider range of quality learning programmes, materials and software.

The architects of such a system must consider the prospect of a TV-based as well as a PC-based network for a number of reasons: (1) TV is almost ubiquitous in UK homes; (2) TV-based systems may be more familiar and popular; (3) the systems may provide cheaper access than PC; (4) the systems allow conditional access and multiple simultaneous users; and (5) the systems are simple to use and unobtrusive when compared to a PC.

The Government recognised this when they stated that the *National Grid for Learning* will, in practical terms, be "promoting flagship learner facilities on the Grid such as digital Interactive TV programming."[7]

4.4 Interview Results. New Considerations

The views expressed by the experts have been collated and analysed, and the results are presented here under broad themes:

Information for Learning

There is a wide belief in the broadcast TV and Interactive TV community that content is king. This is indeed so obvious as to be commonplace. Of course, content is necessary, but in a global information system such as the Internet or an Interactive TV system with hundreds of channels the first problem a learner has is how to find learning opportunities.

Content is only useful if you can access it and utilise it. In the world of Internet or Interactive TV it is as true to say that context is king. While a considerable amount of thought has been put into the *positioning* of services such as banking and shopping there is a feeling that if people want to use the learning services they will seek them out.

The *Electronic Programme Guide* (EPG) is considered one of the "killer apps" in Interactive TV development but its use as an educational tool has not been considered by any of the interviewees. One of the potential educational uses of Interactive TV is to provide information about sources of learning and guidance on how to use them. Simple interactive public information systems such as *Minitel*[8] in France have been very popular and similar systems must be developed for

---

[7] Cf. *Open for Learning, Open for Business. National Grid for Learning.* Online:
   http://www.ngfl.gov.uk
[8] Cf. http://www.minitel.fr

Interactive TV. In addition, there is need for an *Educational Electronic Programme Guide* to guide new learners to learning opportunities.

Content Delivery

Hu (1995) sees mixed-mode learning as one of the defining characteristics of open learning. Interactive TV, in its variety of forms, has the potential to increase and enrich the methods used in not only distance learning but in other forms of education and self-study. One of the simplest ways in which it can do this is as a new medium for content delivery

Here is where the majority of interviewees expect the educational benefits of Interactive TV to lie. They refer to increased quality of content in terms of "CD quality" graphics and "increased interactivity". When forming partnerships to deliver educational or "educative" content they link with educational CD-ROM manufacturers. This can produce some very entertaining and possibly educational content but concentrates too heavily on the Interactive TV system as a means for delivering content while ignoring its potential as a communication and tracking system.

Tracking Systems

The problems of distance learning programmes are often problems of tracking. Compared to tracking, the delivery of educational materials is generally a simple matter and there are many forms of delivery at the disposal of educationalists today.

Methods of tracking a learner from their first interest in learning through registration, enrolment, study, assessment, accreditation and completion are often expensive, time consuming and inflexible. Interactive TV systems are being developed to: (1) cope with large numbers of subscribers; (2) provide conditional access; (3) track the users actions; (4) allow two-way communication between broadcasters and users; and (5) allow two-way communication amongst users.

Unfortunately very few interviewees had considered the use of these sophisticated tracking systems in educational services. As a result the mechanisms that allow such tracking are being developed without any thought for educational use and are often separated, at a system level, from planned educational services.

To cope with large numbers of subscribers, transaction systems are being developed that allow payment for services in a number of ways including subscription, pay per view or token-based systems.

With UK Government plans for "Individual Learning Accounts" these transaction systems may be useful as a method of paying for education. The vast majority of those interviewed do not consider education an important source of revenue and consequently transaction systems are not being tailored for educational services.

The tracking and conditional access mechanisms of Interactive TV systems could allow assessment of students. This is an area that no interviewee has considered. Educational services are thought of as supplementary to traditional study and do not seek to take on any of the tasks necessary to accredit a student.

As educational services are thought of as supplementary to "proper" education there are no plans to evaluate the effectiveness of the services. User tracking and follow-up studies seek to measure "entertainment value" and "satisfaction" rather than to discover whether any real learning has taken place.

Learning Networks

The change in mass and private media began with the invention of print, allowing people to use media individually rather than in a public space. This atomisation is an important theme in both Interactive TV development and distance learning provision. In both cases the emphasis is shifted away from groups towards the individual.

In order to overcome the problems associated with atomisation distance learning provision has moved from concentrating on content towards a learner-centred approach. Recent trends that emphasise the social nature of learning are of interest as they allow increased recognition of the importance of expert networks and peer networks.

Interactive TV technology may allow the development of inexpensive expert networks, which are seen by Hu (1995) as an important part of open learning. Bates (1995) draws a major distinction between one-way and two-way technologies. This distinction is the essential difference between computer-based learning and computer-mediated communication.

From the interviews it appears that the industry is paying most attention to one-way learning technologies with the development of "edutainment" and information services but is not considering the potential of its two-way systems. The exceptions to this general trend are often the most interesting. Interactive TV systems that support multiple users in the same room and encourage interaction between family members as part of their service have been popular.

Accessibility

One of the main themes of the UK government initiatives is that of accessibility. The use of TV has always been considered a good way of making education more accessible through a medium that users are to some degree comfortable with. As viewers tend to watch television throughout their life educational Interactive TV would appear to offer great potential to educationalists concerned with lifelong learning.

Many of those interviewed used the argument of "getting education into the home". However, the problem of access relates most strongly to vocational courses with formal accreditation. There are no plans to offer provision of this sort.

Games, Interactivity, and Learning

The success of the home video game market can be seen as the first appearance of a commercial, mass-market, Interactive TV system (Provenzo 1991; Hertz 1997). The use of digital games in education and their affect on behaviour is a much discussed topic (Dominick 1984; Huff/Collinson 1987; Jones 1984; Jones 1991; Kappes/Thompson 1985; Miller 1984; Papert 1993).

The commercial Interactive TV companies have partly developed from the digital game industry and it is clear that the development practices and user habits that we see in the home digital games market may be very important in the development of Interactive TV in general. Many of the interviewees are of the school of thought that believes that learning should be fun and that games will play an important role in any educational services they provide.

4.5 The US Government and Distance Learning Plans

The US is involved in the construction of an *Advanced National Information Infrastructure* (NII)[9]. The aim is a seamless web of communications networks, computers, databases, and consumer electronics that will put vast amounts of information at users' fingertips. This development has some similarities to the *National Grid for Learning* but is broader in scope. It plans to fulfil the following:

- People could live almost anywhere they wanted, without foregoing opportunities for useful and fulfilling employment, by "telecommuting" to their offices through an electronic highway;

- the best schools, teachers, and courses would be available to all students, without regard to geography, distance, resources, or disability;

- services that improve America's health care system and respond to other important social needs could be available online, without waiting in line, when and where you needed them.

The great promise of *Advanced TV*[10] for the NII comes from some of its technological components: (1) digital signals, that convey picture, sound, text, and data; (2) high resolution screens capable of displaying large amounts of text; (3) two-way interaction between source and viewer.

Donald Norman[11] discusses these advantages:

---

[9] For more information see http://nii.nist.gov/nii/niiinfo.html

[10] An American term that encompasses both *Interactive TV* and *High Definition TV*.

[11] Donald A Norman is Vice President of Advanced Technology at Apple Computer. The quote is from *Advanced TV Standards: into the Future with Jaunty Air and an Anchor Around our Necks*, a paper presented at the IEEE-SMPTE Digital System Information Exchange, Washington DC, August 15, 1995.

To my great surprise, none of these seem to be issues in ATV. Instead, the emphasis has been on entertainment and on the commercial model of current broadcast TV, one in which entertainment titles contain little text, and the sending of data, if it is to be done at all, is one-way, separate from the TV service. Two way interaction, if done at all, is very asymmetric, with the viewer perhaps selecting catalog items or shows, perhaps sending back a credit card number and purchase choice. The notion of symmetric interaction, where some viewers (such as a real estate firm, a High School, or even a private individual) might publish its information for others seems neglected.

Norman's concerns with regard to the US system should be mirrored in Europe.

4.6 Conclusions. Learner Context over Content Delivery

The views that the interviewees have of the consumer are based on services, entertainment and advertising. The systems developed to deliver these can provide much of what is required by an educational system. The views that the interviewees have of education are based on content delivery, "edutainment", and the child learner. Distance learning practice is currently concerned with learner networks, guided discovery, and lifelong learning. The distance learning aims of the UK Government are concerned with vocational learning, encouraging new learners, access to information, and lifelong learning.

There is not a great body of work concerning Interactive TV in general and there is a need for more research in this field. This point has been made by many industry experts including Régis Saint Gerons, Managing Director of *OpenTV*, one of the major Interactive TV platforms in Europe: "The industry is still at a stage where it is developing blindly with little concern for good practice. We need outsiders with no commercial interest to take an informed look."[12]

This need for research and communication underlies the key recommendations made to the European Commission in a recent report.[13]

If Interactive TV-based learning is to become effective we must consider how the systems will change the act of learning itself. It has been said that TV by its very nature trivialises everything it delivers (cf. Postman). How will increased and novel interactivity change this situation and what impact will it have on learning? A student-centred approach needs to be taken to educational Interactive TV in order to guide our use of these powerful new tools.

---

[12] Quoted from an *OpenTV* interview, May 1999, Paris.

[13] Cf. "Development of Satellite and Terrestrial Digital Broadcasting Systems and Services and Implications for Education and Training." PJB Associates. Online:
http://www.ecotec.com/sharedtetriss/news/digitalnewsitem/satellit.htm

It is necessary that educational content designers consider the goals of the commercial developers when entering into partnerships. Education is likely to be seen as either a service or as entertainment and it is up to educationalists to convince developers that education is both and more.

There is need for educational establishments to form partnerships with Interactive TV developers and broadcasters and to become distance learning brokers. There are two reasons why partnerships are necessary: (1) It is not educational bodies but commercial industries that are becoming the gatekeepers of the new communications technologies; (2) in an uncertain future we must be prepared to respond quickly to technological change. I will end with a quote that makes this last point rather neatly: "We cannot be certain of anything in terms of communication technology and education in the future except for the fact that the changes will be far more far-reaching than we anticipate." (cf. British Computer Society 1998).

4.7 References

Bates, A. 1991. *Technology in Open Learning and Distance Education: A Guide for Decision-Makers.* Burnaby, British Columbia: The Commonwealth of Learning, Vancouver and the Open Learning Agency.

Bates, A. 1995. *Technology, Open Learning and Distance Education.* New York: Routledge.

British Computer Society. 1998. *2000 and Beyond: A School Odyssey.* London.

Cairncross, F. 1998. *The Death Of Distance.* London: Orion Business.

Dalkey, D. 1995. "An agenda for the evaluation of distance education." In: D. Sewart (ed.). *One World Many Voices: Quality in Open and Distance Learning.* [Proceedings of the 17th World Conference of the International Council for Distance Education, Oslo] Milton Keynes: Open University.

Dalkey, N. C. 1969. *The Delphi Method: An experimental study of group opinion.* Santa Monica, CA: Rand Corp.

Dominick, J.R. 1984. "Videogames, Television Violence, and Aggression in Teenagers". *Journal of Communication* 34. 136-147.

Hawkridge, D. 1995. "An agenda for the evaluation of distance education". In: D. Sewart (ed.). *One World Many Voices: Quality in Open and Distance Learning.* [Proceedings of the 17th World Conference of the International Council for Distance Education, Oslo] Milton Keynes: Open University.

Hu, Meng-Ching. 1995. "Beyond Distance Teaching Towards Distance Learning: A conceptual Analysis of Transformation Characteristics and Approaches". *Journal of National Chung Cheng University Sec I: Humanities* 27/4. 401-410.

Huff. G., & Collinson F. 1987. "Young Offenders, Gambling and Video Game Playing. A Survey in a Youth Custody Centre". *British Journal of Criminology* 6/1. 325-344.

Jacobs, G./H. Dransfield. 1998. "Scenarios for Interactive TV – Europe's Uncertain Future". *Long Range Planning* 31/3. 396-405.

Jones, G. 1991. "Some Principles of Simulation Design in Interactive Video for Language Instruction". *Simulation & Games* 22/2. 239-247.

Jones, M.B. 1984. "Video Games as Psychological Tests". *Simulation & Games* 15/2. 131-157.

Kappes, B.M./D.L. Thompson. 1985. "Biofeedback versus Video Games: Effects on Impulsivity, Locus of Control and Self-concept with Incarcerated Individuals". *Journal of Clinical Psychology* 41/5. 698-706.

Kaufman, D. 1989. In: R. Sweet (ed.). *Post-Secondary Distance education in Canada: Policies, Practices and Priorities.* Athabasca: Athabasca University/Canadian Society for Studies in Education.

Mason, R. 1998. *Globalising Education: Trends and Applications.* New York: Routledge.

Murray, S. "Rise of Tele-Business in Ireland Gives Jobless in EU New Prospects". *Wall Street Journal Europe*, 5 Febuary 1997.

Nipper, S. 1989. "Third generation distance learning and computer conferencing." In: R. Mason/A. Kaye. *Mindweave: Communication, Computers and Distance Education.* Oxford: Pergamon.

Postman, N. 1985. *Amusing Ourselves to Death.* New York: Penguin.

Schnaars, S. 1989. *Megamistakes.* New York: Free Press.

Stackman, H. 1974. *Delphi Assessment: Expert opinion, forecasting, and group process.* Santa Monica, CA: Rand Corp.

Thornburg, D. *2020 Visions for the Future of Education.* [A report of the Congressional Institute for the Future.] Online:
http://www.tcpd.org/handouts/thornburg/2020visions.html

Wolcott, H.F. 1990. "On seeking — and rejecting — validity in qualitative research". In: E.W. Eisner/A. Peshkin. *Qualitative inquiry in education.* New York: Teachers College Press.

Woodall, P. "A Hitchhiker's Guide to Cybernomics: A Survey of the World Economy". *The Economist,* 28th September 1996.

Contributors

Balcytiene, Aukse (Lithuania)

is Associate Professor and Head of the Department of Journalism as well as Chairwoman of the Graduate School of Journalism at Vytautas Magnus University in Kaunas, Lithuania. She has been involved in a number of internationally funded projects focusing on media and communication prospects. Over the last few years she has been writing about socio-cultural impacts of new media and the role of mass media in post-communist societies.

Bruck, Peter A. (Austria)

is the initiative force behind the EUROPRIX idea and the visionary for its realisation. As Head of the Research Studios Austria at the Austrian Research Centres he forms a network of time-to-market sensitive research groups in the area of e-technologies and multimedia in Austria. In his previous function as chief content manager with the market leading telecom his responsibilities included all operational content business on the Web. Bruck has an outstanding track record as communications researcher and university teacher and he works with a network of other leading experts to develop the European Academy of Digital Media (EAdiM). He is in high demand as speaker on all issues of the new media and the changes in the new economy.

Donaldson, Alan John M. (UK)

is Visiting Academic at Middlesex University School of Computing Science. Since 1999 he has worked on a project on "systems failures".

Kopper, Gerd G. (Germany)

is Professor at the Institute of Journalism at the University of Dortmund, where he developed the "Euro-Journalism" module and operates closely with the Erich-Brost-Institute of Journalism in Europe founded in 1991. In his work Gerd G. Kopper aims at encouraging European journalism both practically and theoretically.

Mandea, Nicolae (Romania)

studied and works at the University of Drama and Cinematography (Universitatea Nationala de Arta Teatrala si Cinematografica) in Bucharest, Romania.

Mindruta, Denisa (Romania)

studied and works at the University of Drama and Cinematography (Universitatea Nationala de Arta Teatrala si Cinematografica) in Bucharest, Romania.

Nolan, Stuart (UK)

is the founder of Needlework TV, an Interactive TV education and training company. He is a consultant on Interactive TV to a number of companies and government initiatives and was previously Interactive TV Consultant for Oyster Partners and a research fellow in Interactive TV and Learning at Manchester Metropolitan University. Stuart has been working in Interactive TV since the mid-Nineties producing enhanced versions of over 20 commercial TV shows.

Picard, Robert G. (USA/Finland)

is Professor at the Business Research and Development Centre, Media Group at the Turku School of Economics and Business Administration. Research activities of the Media Group focus on printing and publishing, broadcasting, advertising, new media, and copyright issues.

Svirmieckiene, Dalia (Lithuania)

studied at Vytautas Magnus University (VMU) in Kaunas, Lithuania, and works in the Multimedia Lab of VMU.

Taylor, Paul A. (UK)

is Lecturer in the Sociology of Technology at the Institute for Social Research at the University of Salford, UK. His current research interests concentrate on the politics and culture of the Information Age.

Vitiello, Guiseppe (Italy/France)

is in charge of the "Electronic Publishing, Books and Archives"-Project of the Council of Europe in Strasbourg, France. Earlier he held positions as Lecturer in Italian and Linguistics at the Universities of Toulouse and Orléans and as Assistant to the Director of the National Library of Florence. He is the author of various publications and reports on the history of culture and translation and in the library and information field.

Author Index